Louisiana Notary Exam
Sample Questions and Answers
2022

LOUISIANA NOTARY EXAM
SAMPLE QUESTIONS AND ANSWERS
2022

Explanations Keyed to the Official Study Guide

Steven Alan Childress

QUID PRO BOOKS
New Orleans, Louisiana

Copyright © 2022 by Steven Alan Childress. All rights reserved. No part of this book including only the sample questions may be reproduced, in any form including scanning the text or copying digital or ebook files, without written permission by the publisher.

Published in 2022 by Quid Pro Books. Second trade paperback printing: May, 2022.

ISBN 978-1-61027-450-0 (trade paperback)
ISBN 978-1-61027-451-7 (ePUB)
ISBN 978-1-61027-449-4 (mass market paperback)

QUID PRO BOOKS
5860 Citrus Blvd., Suite D
New Orleans, Louisiana 70123
www.quidprobooks.com

This information is provided to aid comprehension of the Louisiana notary examination and its official study guide, and to facilitate practice and preparation for the exam. It is unofficial, is not a product of the Louisiana Secretary of State or LSU, and is based on public information about the exam. It should not be construed as legal advice or the practice of law. Please consult an attorney for inquiries regarding legal matters. For information on how to contact the author about this book, see the *About the Author* section at the end; corrections are welcome.

Publisher's Cataloging-in-Publication

Childress, Steven Alan.

    Louisiana notary exam sample questions and answers 2022 : explanations keyed to the official Study Guide / Steven Alan Childress.

        p. cm.

    Includes explanations and page references.

    Series: *Self-Study Sherpa Series*, #7

1. Notaries. 2. Notaries—United States. 3. Notaries—Louisiana. 4. Notaries—Louisiana—Handbooks, Manuals, etc. I. Title. II. Series.

KF8797 .C48 2022   2022708936

Cover design copyright © 2022 by Quid Pro, LLC. The Self-Study Sherpa Series image of the munching mountain goat, *Sherpa*, is a trademark of Quid Pro, LLC, with original artwork © by Mary Ruth Pruitt, used by permission and with the thanks of the publisher.

Contents

1 • Introduction: The Exam and Study Resources 1

2 • How This is Like, and Unlike, the State Exam 3

3 • Ways to Split Up These Exams if You Want to 7

4 • Library Document for Exam A 9

5 • Exam A 11

6 • Library Document for Exam B 23

7 • Exam B 25

8 • Library Document for Exam C 37

9 • Exam C 39

10 • Mini-Exam D 53

11 • Answers and Explanations: Exam A 63

12 • Answers and Explanations: Exam B 75

13 • Answers and Explanations: Exam C 87

14 • Answers and Explanations: Mini-Exam D 101

15 • Exam Strategies 107

16 • Your Notes 113

About the author 115

Louisiana Notary Exam
Sample Questions and Answers
2022

1

Introduction: The Exam and Study Resources

STOP. Please don't flip through the book and read a lot of questions before you scan this introduction. Seeing too much of it may lessen its usefulness to simulate an exam or two for yourself after you've prepared well for the state exam. I'll detail below why I say this, but first, a little on the exam and this book.

The Louisiana state notary examination is famously challenging, usually sporting below a 20% pass rate at each administration. Everything you need to know to pass is found somewhere in the state's official study guide, *Fundamentals of Louisiana Notarial Law and Practice*, which is interesting, detailed, and available to use open-book the day of the exam—so it's certainly a helpful resource for preparing and taking the exam itself. But it's 700 pages long, dense, not intuitively organized, and without an index. Most people find the book—and of course the subject-matter of notary law itself—to be a challenge even before game day.

To that end, over thirty prep courses—in-person, online, or some combination—have been registered with the state and are listed on the Secretary of State's website. Some community colleges and universities offer academic courses in notary law and practice, such as one I teach at Tulane's School of Professional Advancement.* Many effective study aids including detailed workbooks and outlines are available, as are private study groups and Facebook groups for support. I've published a book of information on the exam, study strategies, and big-picture discussions of key areas of law. Its current edition is entitled *Louisiana Notary Exam Sidepiece to the 2022 Study Guide: Tips, Index, Forms—Essentials Missing in the Official Book*.

All of these resources recommend reviewing sample questions and even taking practice exams, and the best classes and workbooks do provide exam-taking. The state's *Fundamentals* book includes a mini-test in the back. This book is not meant to obviate further advice and sample questions that you get by taking a class or self-prepping with quality commercial notebooks that include quizzes. My goal is to support and augment those resources, not wholly replace them (heaven forbid my own class), since many students do need organized study or outlines to have a good shot at passing the exam.

---

* In addition to full-length prep courses, shorter introductory or review classes are available. My wife Michele and I, for example, offer webinars in both live and recorded formats, via Zoom. An introductory one is called "The Big Picture," while a post-study review and practice-exam workshop is "The Final Lap" (including a practice exam of 30 questions different from this book's), seen at www.notarysidepiece.com. A month before the state exam, Fred Davis usually offers an in-person review and workshop in Lafayette. And other experienced instructors, such as Ronda Gabb, Shane Milazzo, and Jenn Brown, may offer review classes or recordings close in time to the exam.

But full-length classes cost a lot of money and may come at times that don't fit a working schedule—or they already started before the time seemed right to prep for the next exam. We saw the need for a workbook wholly devoted to sample questions while then adding detailed explanations of the options and answers, cross-referenced to the official study guide. We priced it relatively low so that there's room in the budget for other resources.

This book's explanations and page references are keyed specifically to the 2022 (purple) *Fundamentals* guide and, occasionally where warranted, to the new 2022 edition of *Sidepiece*. The Secretary of State website has not announced for the rest of this year any changes to the structure, scope, and rules of the exams to be administered in 2022 or the format of the individual questions one can anticipate. Sample questions based on that format predictably apply for this year, and really for the near future until that office announces a major change. In terms of the scheduling of 2022 exams—which has been volatile and shifting lately as the SOS dealt with pandemic and hurricanes—keep an eye on the SOS site for announcements of test dates and possible last-minute changes.

This book isn't sponsored by the Secretary of State, or LSU's testing office which administers the notary exam several times a year for the SOS. It's unofficial and based on publicly available information. But I've been teaching and testing on law for 35 years; took the state-wide notary exam; practice as a notary with my wife Michele; and give, grade, and explain several multiple-choice exams in my notary class. This is my best view of the format, coverage, and phrasing of the typical question one may face on the state exam—while explaining the strategy or "trick" behind several questions that are like a decoy you may face in the official test. It's good practice.

Why the "**STOP**" above? As I see it, there are two ways to use this book. First, *wait*, and use it as review and exam-practice after your own thorough preparation for the exam—after you've read *Fundamentals* and used whatever study aids or classwork to get ready. Or, second, use it as a learning tool *as you go*—though, even then, it's best to have enough reading under your belt that the questions and explanations make sense. The order here is fairly random to mimic the real exam, and not so much centered on specific subjects like "donations" as other guides do it. It can replicate a time-pressured exam scenario or it can be lighter reading, depending on your comfort level for simulating the state exam and the timeframe in which you decide to use this. Also, you could read one test (or part of it) before full study, then wait to use the other ones as a proper measure of your preparation and exam skills, taking those at least under simulated exam conditions and proper time limits. I would recommend, in that case, test A as the prep one and hold off on B, C, and D until later. Chapter 3 guides you in breaking down the exams further, if you prefer to employ them in smaller chunks.

However you approach it, don't read the answers and explanations before truly thinking about the questions on their own and trying to answer them by looking through *Fundamentals*. That's the practice you need. Don't be Michele, who six minutes into *Dateline*, grabs her phone and then announces Justin did it.

2

How This is Like, and Unlike, the State Exam

My firm belief is that—whatever else you do, including these practice questions—the best prep for the exam includes reading *Fundamentals* thoroughly, handwriting an index and extra cross-references into it, knowing most-tested subjects and recent changes to notary law, and focusing on exam strategies and tips peculiar to the current format of the state exam. That's all in my other book and I don't rehash all of it here, though the Explanations chapters offer many tactics (in text boxes), as does ch. 15 below, "Exam Strategies."

This book's main focus is on potential questions and answers. It's organized into three separate tests of 36 to 39 questions each, each like *half* of the actual exam (they test on 72 to 80 questions in five hours). Plus there's a mini-exam of 18 questions, equaling 1/4 of the state exam. All questions have four answer choices, with the occasional few having five—just like the state exam does it, too. They don't give two-option T/F questions.

Though there are some larger subject groupings within each test, as with the real one, here the questions tend to be even more broad and random than it may seem on exam day—to provide more reach and coverage than if we just had two larger subjects per test, such as "Mandates" or "Trusts." Theirs is likely to have five sets of some fifteen questions, using such commanding, succinct headings. But the grouping system of their exam works out more randomly than it *looks:* a section called "Small Successions" may ask questions far-afield from their ch. 27 on that, instead covering "things," separate property, affidavits, and clauses. A grouping called "Testaments" may include trusts and notary practice. One way the exam is hard is the answer may be found in the "wrong" chapter if you go by the subject headings in the exam.

In any event, we use smaller and more explicitly diverse groupings than you'll get on the real exam. And their questions may refer to more, or fewer, "library documents" that they provide on the side, compared to ours (while some administrations may use mostly scenarios and few if any source documents).

Another way these sample exams may differ from the official one is that they probably are more uniformly difficult, and not just because they are a bit more randomly dispersed. The examiners apparently do not attempt to normalize each question—make each one as hard as the others. They have several questions which are straightforward and answered right out of the book (like knowing the seal is your signature, or the magic words of a jurat), in a place pretty easy to locate if you've read it. The low-hanging fruit is there for the picking. Some of the questions in this book emulate that level of difficulty, but even then with, I suspect, a little more reading than the examiners use in some of theirs.* It's more educational to teach the harder formats and subjects than the ones most people will get right anyway. So, these questions do.

Another way these questions may seem a bit harder is that more of them are a continuation of the question before, whereas the examiners may try to make several questions more independent so they can be given in a different order. They tend to use scenarios and base questions off of that in a rolling way, but perhaps not as often as here.

To that end, if you do the math after taking one of these tests or part of one, don't take your percentage score too seriously. It's not meant to be a prediction of their official scoring, though it may well be a useful wake-up call. I would guess the score here would predict a lower number than you'd get for a comparable performance on the actual exam, plus they scale their passing score to some extent after reviewing all the exams.

If you decide to score the exams to use as a measuring stick, if not a predictor, a fair estimate is that getting 60–65% consistently right is a very good start and can be improved by reviewing the answers and explanations. Less than 45% isn't great, and suggests buckling down to know the study guide better—and adding an index to it if you view the biggest problem as not *finding* the answers in the place you looked. Hopefully most of your issue is exam-taking technique and getting confused by the question formats, which is fixed by more practice and recognizing the twists they often use in them. That's what this book explains.

One way some of our questions may be somewhat easier is that we try to resolve ambiguity as much as possible, while the actual exam at least *feels* as if it's occasionally ambiguous on purpose. For example, we tend to preface a question with "assuming the act is otherwise valid, . . ." while the actual questions may leave that out and you apparently are supposed to answer focusing only on the choices they give you in *that* question (when maybe the best answer should be "none of these choices make the act valid because all the other things you did to it above make it unfixable"). Again, I assume they do that because they rearrange questions and can't always say "in the preceding question, now assume X." Still, these questions in format and phrasing are, as far as possible, representative.

Related, we rely less on the format of having two "right" answers where you're supposed to pick the "best"—here, using less of the "good but not best" format they are *said* to use. Because of their exam disclaimer (the top of the first page says to pick the "best"), they apparently don't feel the need to take the "tricky" out of answer choices as long as they feel comfortable with the "more right" answer. But we strive to make one answer right and the others wrong, even if

---

* Some are as easy as knowing the signature is the seal. One could instead test it with an involved scenario making it also about keeping parties straight—an essential test skill to get in the habit of—whereas the examiners could ask it in a declarative way, for instance, "The notary's seal is his or her: A. Signature. B. Stamp. C. Embosser. D. Official wall license or notary identification card." To foster more practice in scenario-unpacking and keeping facts straight, we frame many in the form of a scenario rather than a simple declaration.

that's just for some technical or picky reason (found in the book). Still, I firmly believe that's more like the actual exam than most people *feel* when leaving the exam: they *think* there are two right answers for a lot of questions. Yet I suspect if you had more time to dig into the book you'd reduce it to only one right option of the four or five offered, even if the reason is minor or found in an unexpected place in the book.

Other workbooks seem to offer questions with one actual correct answer and not just a guess between two good ones, and I feel they're right to do so. Ultimately, a fair exam is one where the right answer is consistently so, not missed by people who prepped well for the exam and understand the question.

While the individual questions on the official exam may range from easy to Einstein, the state examiners *do* work hard to normalize the exam *as a whole* by making each administration about as hard as others before it. They apparently reuse norm-tested questions (or similar ones). They don't want the August exam to be perceived as much easier than June. But we have not normalized these questions or the four exam sets: one test may be somewhat tougher than the others (please let us know). It's supposed to be good practice, not a perfect predictor. The main goal is to answer the questions as best you can—then not only reaffirm what you get right, but learn from what you did "wrong," as explained below in ch. 11–14. Hopefully in the process it feels affirming and supportive, but most of all the challenge this book presents should not be disheartening, just as the *Fundamentals* text should not be overwhelming. Our hope is that providing detailed explanations and tactics takes the panic out of the exam.

Finally, no attempt is made here to be comprehensive as to the entire state study guide. But our exams likely cover far more ground than any one state test does, in order to be useful as a review exercise. Your actual exam may have a group of fifteen questions (or zero) entitled "Business Entities" or "Titled Vehicles" and thus test one specific chapter a lot (ch. 28 or 23, for those titles).

It'd be lucky for you if most of the answers to that section can be found in the named chapter for it. It happens—but don't count on it. As noted above, they may just use the title to group together several questions only loosely related to the obvious guide chapter. A "business" section may have questions on whether an LLC can be a trustee (so, ch. 25) or what its form of appearance or signature would look like (ch. 19). A car-title section could use that as a springboard to ask not just about info in ch. 23, but also about ownership of things generally (ch. 8), security devices to finance movables (ch. 17), and contrasting the act of correction for a vehicle with the authentic act used to fix clerical errors in a sale of an immovable, located in ch. 29 and App. A. (This is why cross-referencing and indexing are so important.) In any event, the following questions try to emulate that springboard approach, too, to be most representative of what you can expect on the official notary public exam.

3

Ways to Split Up These Exams if You Want to

Exams A, B, and C are presented each as 36 to 39 questions, replicating half the length and time you'll have on the actual state-administered one. There's one bonus mini-exam (D) with 18 questions, so one-quarter of a typical full exam. Chapter 1 (p. 2) discussed whether you should wait to take these exams until you've studied far into the process, and that's probably best; but maybe your preferred method of study is to use some of these before you're at that stage.

If you'd like to self-test or review in smaller chunks than half an exam (at whatever stage of preparedness), here are some suggestions on dividing them into shorter tests—with the split based in part on the goal of minimizing overlap of subject matter, to give you more coverage for each partial task. Of course, you could break it down even further by taking each section heading within an exam on its own. But the following breakdown is more true to the heft of the state-administered exam, and is more evenly distributed to practice time-management skills.

For a smaller version of an exam, ideally you'd give yourself no more than four minutes per question (or total minutes of four times the number of questions). But for practice purposes, and using smaller chunks that don't allow you to "get rolling" like you will when deeper into the actual exam, it wouldn't be unrealistic or unhelpful to make it five or six minutes per question.

EXAM A

- Combine Section 1 (questions 1–10) and Sections 4 and 5 (questions 30–37) into one exam of 18 questions. This might be entitled "Notary Practice and Conveyances."

- Combine Sections 2 and 3 (questions 11–29) into one exam of 19 questions. This may be "Affidavits and Testaments."

EXAM B

- Section 1 (questions 1–20) as one exam of 20 questions.

- Section 2 (questions 21–36) as one exam of 16 questions.

EXAM C

- Sections 1 (questions 1–9) and 2 (questions 11–20) as one exam of 20 questions.

- Sections 3 (questions 21–28), 4 (questions 29–34), and 5 (questions 35–

39) as one exam of 19 questions.

EXAM D
- Sections 1 (questions 1–5), 2 (questions 6–11), and 3 (questions 12–18) as one exam of 18 questions.

4

Library Document for Exam A

During the Secretary of State's exam, the library document(s) on which a set of questions is based (more or less) are given to you as a separate handout you can flip through and write on during the exam.

This is the library to refer to, for some of the questions in Exam A. In all libraries, a line with an x on it is actually signed there. The x is not just a place where the signature goes; consider it to be signed.

<u>File 1 consists of the following document:</u>

AFFIDAVIT OF NAME CHANGE BY MARRIAGE

STATE OF LOUISIANA

[A] PARISH OF ORLEANS

BEFORE ME, the undersigned notary public, duly qualified in the State of Louisiana and commissioned in the Parish of Union, came and appeared

[B] Miley Cyrus, who is of the age of majority and domiciled in the Parish of Lafayette,

[C] who hereby affirms, deposes, and states:

Pursuant to Article 100 of the Louisiana Civil Code, that she does by these presents hereby adopt the surname of her spouse, Liam Hemsworth, to whom she was married on December 28, 2018, and is, therefore, one and the same person as MILEY RAE HEMSWORTH and signs both signatures below for identification.

[D] THUS DONE, READ AND SIGNED at _____ **[E]** _____, Louisiana, on June 7, 2020.

____x_____ ____x_____
Cardi B. Smith   **[F]** Miley Cyrus, Appearer

____x_____ ____x_____
Roberta Flack   **[G]** Miley Ray Hemsworth, Appearer

_____x_____
Chris Hemsworth, Notary Public
Notary ID #55555

5

Exam A

Number of questions: 37 | Time limit: 2 hours, 40 minutes

Section 1 • Notarial Practice and the Louisiana System

1. A notary is convicted of misdemeanor assault from a bar fight (committed on a day off from working as a mobile notary). She is sentenced to one month of home confinement. After serving this sentence, will the notary be subject to suspension?

A. No, because only misfeasance or dereliction of duty such as misfiling documents or injuring the public record is grounds for suspension.

B. Yes, because conviction of a crime, serious enough to get actual confinement and not just a suspended sentence, allows the Secretary of State to suspend the notary.

C. No, because crimes unrelated to the notarial function must amount to a felony before suspension or revocation is warranted.

D. Yes, because conviction of a crime, serious enough to get actual confinement and not just a suspended sentence, allows the district court (in the parish where the notary is commissioned) to suspend the notary.

2. Which of the following is considered to be the supreme source of law in the Louisiana civil law system?

A. Attorney General Opinions

B. constitutional ancillaries

C. judicial opinions of the Louisiana Supreme Court

D. legislation

3. Which of the following is considered to be a valid function of the Louisiana civil law notary?

A. drafting and attesting to such juridical acts as affidavits, witness acknowledgments, authentic acts, and acts of correction

B. advising clients on whether to include a provision in a will that would make the named executor be appointed as independent and without the requirement of posting bond

C. conducting a family meeting to explain the legal process and forms by which one of them could adopt a three-year-old who has been orphaned by the death of their relatives (the parents of the child)

D. all of the above

4. An act in derogation of laws for the protection of the public interest is considered to be:

A. relatively null

B. enforceable only by a court of appellate jurisdiction

C. absolutely null

D. enforceable only by a court of original jurisdiction

5. Which of the following statement is false?

A. The Mayor's Court cannot conduct jury trials.

B. The Civil Code of Louisiana has several "books," including one dealing with conflict of laws added more recently than the others.

C. The judicial hierarchy of the Louisiana court system makes the Court of Appeal higher than the Mayor's Court.

D. The Louisiana Supreme Court does not have "original jurisdiction," which is for trials.

6. A notary, Bill, works part-time for the bank while his wife, Wanda, is sole manager of a car dealership. The bank that employs Bill provides loans for customers to purchase cars, including cars bought from Wanda's workplace. May Bill properly serve as notary for the transactions involving Wanda's dealership?

A. No, because Bill is a stockholder, director, officer, of a bank which is party to an instrument related to Wanda's work.

B. Yes, because he has no direct personal interest in these transactions.

C. No, because in a community property jurisdiction, Wanda's work necessarily raises an interest in Bill, such that it is an example of self-dealing.

D. Yes, because it is unlikely that a dissatisfied customer of the car dealership would be able to question the credibility of the notary and his spouse.

7. An authentic act entered into by a corporation contains the following clause:

Three Rivers Corporation, a Louisiana Business Corporation domiciled in Vernon Parish, Louisiana, Taxpayer ID number 84-1221370, herein represented by Charles Wise, President, acting by virtue of a resolution of the board of directors adopted on December 22, 2014, a copy of which is attached and incorporated herein by reference.

This clause is an example of:

A. conclusion

B. appearance

C. preamble

D. business entity

8. In the preceding example, how would the act's signature line be worded?

A. Charles Wise, individually and as President for Three Rivers Corporation

B. Charles Wise, President, on behalf of Three Rivers Corporation

C. Three Rivers Corporation, by and through Charles Wise, President

D. all of the above are effective in the example given

E. either B or C but not A is effective in the example given

9. In the above example, assuming the original clause in #7 is used and is valid, how might Charles establish his authority to sign the act?

A. It is automatically established as long as the corporation's public information at the Secretary of State's website states that Charles is president of Three Rivers Corporation.

B. It is established by attaching a Corporate Resolution by the board of directors, which document must be in authentic form.

C. It is established by recording in the appropriate public record a Corporate Resolution by the board of directors.

D. It is established by attaching a Corporate Resolution by the board of directors, which document need not be in authentic form.

E. Either C or D is effective in the example given.

10. Which of the following is a thing or interest that the owner cannot finance with a mortgage?

A. a usufruct of farm land

B. a certificate of deposit worth $10,000

C. a condominium

D. a house owned by a trustee of a Louisiana trust

Section 2 • Name Change by Marriage

*Using the document shown as **File 1** in our Library, answer the following questions.*

SCENARIO: Assume for all questions below, unless otherwise stated, that the caption correctly states the proper form for an act of this kind.

11. All of the following would be acceptable and appropriate alternative captions to this instrument, except:

A. Affidavit of One and the Same

B. Authentic Act of Name Change

C. Affidavit of Distinction

D. Declaration of Name Change by Marriage

12. Given the document's stated purpose and the form noted in the caption, which of the following statements is false?

A. It is not necessary for the document to be in authentic form.

B. Lines F and G in the document could properly say "Affiant" in place of "Appearer."

C. The document is not wholly necessary as a legal matter because changes to the surname are automatic upon marriage unless a spouse opts out.

D. The document is not wholly necessary as a practical matter because a married person is permitted to use the surname of her or his spouse.

13. Given the document's stated purpose and the form noted in the caption, and assuming line E is filled in correctly as "Lafayette," which of the following statements is incomplete or misstated to have the intended legal effect?

A. Clause B

B. Clause C

C. Clause D

D. Both Clause C and Clause D are incomplete or misstated

14. Assume for this question only that Miley arrives to the notary having signed lines F and G before, at her home. Chris administers an oath and asks Miley whether those are her signatures and sworn facts, and she affirms to him that they are. Does the document have legal effect?

A. Yes, because Miley personally appeared before him, took the oath, and confirmed the testimony and that she signed it.

B. No, because then the notary has committed injury to the public record by verifying that the document was signed in his presence when it was not.

C. No, because of the "de facto" doctrine, which requires that civil law courts interpret words literally and enforce documents that have lived up to the formalities required.

D. Yes, but only if she signs the document again in his presence.

15. Assuming the caption, venue clause, and the clause stated in paragraph B are otherwise correct, which of the following is false?

A. Line E should not read "Shreveport" (which is a city in Caddo Parish).

B. Only one person should sign as affiant in either line F or G, but not both

C. Line B may correctly say "Parish of Lafayette" even though she spends more than 180 days of the year on the road in concerts and film projects.

D. Line E should not read "Lafayette" (which is a city in Lafayette Parish).

16. Assume that Liam and Chris are brothers. Which of the following statements is true?

A. It is improper for Chris to act as notary in this matter because of his conflict of interest involving having Liam as his brother and Miley as his sister-in-law.

B. It would be proper for Chris to act as notary in this matter, if the signing will take place outside of Union Parish, assuming he lacks state-wide jurisdiction because he became a notary public in 2003.

C. It is proper for Chris to serve as notary in this matter only because Liam is merely named in the document and is not a signator.

D. It is proper for Chris to serve as notary in this matter because he has no personal interest.

17. The first part of Clause D (in all caps):

A. is correctly stated as is

B. should be replaced by the evidence of oath

C. should quote as "substantially similar" as possible the statutory attestation language of Civil Code art. 1577

D. should be replaced by the jurat

18. Which of the following statements is true?

A. This document would legally fail if it turns out that only one witness signed it, because juridical acts must be done in authentic form.

B. It is advisable that Cardi B. Smith and Roberta Flack not be related to each other.

C. This document would legally fail if it turns out that Miley signed it without a notary present (but with Cardi B. Smith and Roberta Flack signing it with her), and then Cardi went to the notary Chris and executed a proper witness acknowledgment.

D. This form of juridical act requires, either on line C or D, that Miley expressly accept that it is made "under penalty of perjury" in the event she is lying.

19. Assume for this question that Chris's commission, at the time of signing of this document, had been suspended because he recently failed to file an annual report with the Secretary of State. Later the report is filed and the commission is reinstated. Chris was not aware of this deficiency at time of signing, nor had the Secretary of State provided information yet about the suspension. Is the document likely to be considered valid?

A. No, because the civil law reads strictly all formal requirements such as a duly commissioned notary.

B. Yes, because Louisiana law may apply the "de facto" doctrine to protect the innocent parties in such situations.

C. No, because the annual report would have revealed to the parties the current parish of commission for the notary public, which they are entitled to know.

D. Yes, because the presence of the two witnesses guarantees that Miley really signed it.

20. Assume that the notary Chris is a legal resident of Louisiana but a citizen only of Australia. His commission would be invalid for all the following reasons except:

A. He does not have a high school diploma or equivalent such as the GED.

B. He is not currently a resident of the Parish of Union where he holds his commission.

C. He is not registered to vote in the Parish of Union where he holds his commission.

D. He has not posted a bond or equivalent surety to protect the governor in the event of mistakes he may make as a notary.

21. Miley owns a condo in Claiborne Parish that she bought in 2016 with her own funds and has not, since the marriage, made it part of the legal regime with Liam. In 2020, she began to collect fees from short-term rentals of the condo. Which of the following statements is false?

A. Miley may use the rental fees however she wants because they are her separate property.

B. Liam may execute an authentic act to convey his community interest in the rental fees to Miley.

C. The rental fees are considered a fruit of her separate property earned during the marriage and thus are part of the community.

D. Miley may reserve the fees by an acknowledged act declaring them to be separate property, as long as she provides a copy to Liam as notice and files the original for registry in Claiborne Parish.

22. Assume for this question that Miley's condo in Claiborne Parish is owned by her with a usufruct in favor of her father, Billy. In the act establishing the usufruct, she stated no time limit. Who owns the rental fees earned on the condo when it is used for short-term rentals?

A. Billy owns the fees.

B. Billy and Miley share ownership of the fees.

C. Miley owns the fees.

D. Miley and Liam share ownership of the fees.

23. Billy lives in the condo under his usufruct, as in the preceding question. What fees or expenses is he responsible for?

A. condo fees paid monthly to keep up the common areas and provide security

B. property tax levied by Claiborne Parish

C. costs of ordinary repairs to keep the condo in good condition

D. all of the above

24. In the preceding question, assume Miley dies. Does Billy still have the right to live in the condo?

A. Yes, up until ten years from execution of the act of usufruct, if that time extends past Miley's death.

B. No, the usufruct terminates at the time of Miley's death.

C. Yes, because the right of habitation is inheritable.

D. No, because Liam's usufruct as a surviving spouse replaces Billy's legal usufruct.

E. None of the above is correct.

Section 3 • Testaments

SCENARIO: Cal Cook asks a notary (Katrina Katz) to draft a testament in which all of his belongings are left to his friend Roger upon his death, to the exclusion of his two natural children (Jan, aged 24, and Nan, 26), who do not have any disabilities. Cal makes his home in only one place, in Baton Rouge (East Baton Rouge Parish), but plans to sign the completed instrument in New Orleans (Orleans Parish), if that is allowed as a place to sign. Cal wants to sign it on March 3, 2020; the testament is two pages long. The notary was commissioned in Caddo Parish after passing the state-wide notary exam in 2014.

25. May Cal Cook sign the testament in New Orleans?

A. Yes, if he owns property there.

B. Yes, because Katrina has state-wide jurisdiction, which allows appearers in her acts to sign anywhere.

C. Yes, because there is no requirement for an appearer to sign in their parish of domicile.

D. Yes, if he intends for the testament to be probated in Orleans Parish.

26. May Jan and Nan be left out of a legacy, giving everything in a succession to Roger? (Assume at the time of Cal's death and after, that they continue to not be disabled.)

A. Nan and Jan are forced heirs and will be granted a portion of the estate in the succession.

B. Jan is a forced heir and will be granted a portion of the estate in the succession; Nan is not a forced heir.

C. Neither Jan nor Nan is considered an "heir" because Cal has a valid testament; thus, they are "legatees."

D. Neither Jan nor Nan is a forced heir, so the entire estate may be left to Roger.

27. In the above testament, after the testator's signature portion of the will (his signature line and full name printed out), which of the following statements should be added, to make it valid?

A. This testament consisting of two (2) pages has been prepared and printed under my direction by Katrina Katz, Notary Public, for execution in accordance with the notarial testament law of this state, La. C.C. arts. 1576, et seq.

B. In our presence the testator has declared or signified that this instrument is his testament and has signed it at the end and on each other separate page, and in the presence of the testator and each other we have hereunto subscribed our names, this 3rd day of March, 2020 at New Orleans, LA.

C. In our presence the testator has declared or signified that this instrument is his testament and has signed it at the end and on each other separate page, and in the presence of the testator and each other we have hereunto subscribed our names, this 3rd day of March, 2020 at Baton Rouge, LA.

D. This testament consisting of two (2) pages has been prepared and printed under my direction by Katrina Katz, Notary Public, for execution in accordance with the notarial testament law of this state, La. C.C. arts. 1576, et seq., and is hereunto executed in Caddo Parish.

28. Assume in the preceding question that one of the clauses is used which dates the instrument as March 3 and is proper. It is easy to establish from external events that it was in fact signed March 3. But the preamble from an earlier draft says February 29, 2020. Which of the following statements is true?

A. The testament is valid even with the error, given the ready resolution by using external facts to fix the correct date it was signed.

B. The testament may be made valid after everyone has signed simply by having Katrina correct the date in the preamble in her handwriting and initial next to it.

C. The testament may be made valid after everyone has signed simply by having Cal correct the date in the preamble in his handwriting and initial next to it.

D. The testament is invalid because of the discrepancy, given that it now appears that the first page is just a draft and may not capture the intentions of the testator.

29. Katrina prints the testament double-sided on one sheet of paper. Roger executes it, signing only in the usual place after his dispositions. Is the testament valid?

A. The testament is valid because it is now considered one page and has been signed on the page; the policy preventing substitution of pages by someone other than the testator is not thwarted.

B. The testament is valid because it is now considered one page and has been signed on the page; the jurisprudence applies a literal definition of "page" and here there is in fact one page.

C. The testament is invalid as a matter of law because the testator's signature is required on both sides of the page; the jurisprudence has made clear that the side of the page that is not signed must at least be initialed if the document is double-sided.

D. The testament is invalid as a matter of law because the testator's signature is required on both sides of the page; the jurisprudence has made clear that each side of the page must be signed if the document is double-sided.

Section 4 • Agreement to Pet Care

SCENARIO: Joy is agreeing in writing with Stan for him to take care of Joy's cat for two weeks as a trade-off for Joy's keeping Stan's fish for a month later in the year.

30. This is an example of:

A. counterletter

B. exchange

C. strictly personal obligations

D. pet trust

31. In the previous question, they want the document accomplishing this agreement to be executed in such a way that it can be introduced in court without needing witnesses to authenticate the document for admission into evidence. They can do this by:

A. Private act.

B. Authentic act.

C. Acknowledged act.

D. All of the above.

E. Either B or C but not A.

32. In the previous situation, assume that they sign the document at Stan's home. Joy takes the document to a notary to have it received. Which of the following could not accomplish the goal stated in the previous question?

A. While Joy is at the notary's office, Stan arrives, and they both sign the document again in the presence of two witnesses; the witnesses then sign in the appropriate place, followed by the notary.

B. Joy signs it before the notary, who puts it aside. Later, Stan arrives at the notary separately and signs it before the notary, who then signs it as well.

C. Joy had two witnesses sign the original document along with Stan and herself, and one of those witnesses goes to the notary and executes an affidavit stating that the original document was signed by Stan and Joy.

D. Joy expressly and in a signed writing recognizes her own signature on the document, in the presence of two witnesses and the notary, who then sign it as well.

33. In the original scenario, involving a trade of services for pet care, assume that Stan and Joy further sign a separate, private act that clarifies that Stan's "fish" is their private code for his collection of (illegal) weapons that he doesn't want to get stolen. This separate act is an example of:

A. counterletter

B. exchange

C. strictly personal obligation

D. prohibited vulgar substitution

34. In the previous question, assume Joy and Stan sign the separate document to accomplish their clarification. A court refuses to enforce the agreement. This decision is based on:

A. recognizing that such clarifications that deviate from the normally understood terms of the original agreement are disfavored.

B. recognizing that the private act is a relative nullity.

C. recognizing that such clarifications that deviate from the normally understood terms of the original agreement must be notarized.

D. recognizing that the private act is an absolute nullity.

Section 5 • Donations and Things

35. Amy transfers to her friend Bill a plot of land in Caddo Parish. The document stating this includes the phrase that this is done "because he has voluntarily worked, and keeps working, on the land for years to keep it up, and that is roughly worth what this plot is worth." The document is stated correctly and properly notarized at the bottom by a commissioned notary with state-wide jurisdiction. But no witnesses were present. Is the document valid despite their absence?

A. No, because this is a donation inter vivos that must be in authentic form.

B. Yes, because this is a remunerative donation.

C. Yes, because this is an onerous donation.

D. Yes, because by estimating the value of the plot, she has made it a dation en paiement.

36. From the facts given in the previous question, assume for this question that Bill also was not present at the signing, and the document does not have a space for him to sign. Assume it is proper that no witnesses signed it. Is the donation valid?

A. Immediately so, because the document is signed and notarized.

B. Yes, in the future once Bill takes out a mortgage on the property and files that mortgage in Caddo Parish.

C. Yes, in the future once Bill has accepted in writing.

D. Both B and C are correct.

37. The city of Monroe buys several fire trucks for its stations. The trucks are considered to be:

A. private things

B. common things

C. civil fruits

D. public things

STOP. END EXAM A.

6

Library Document for Exam B

This is the library to refer to, for some of the questions in Exam B. In all libraries, a line with an x on it is actually signed there. The x is not just a place where the signature goes; consider it to be signed.

<u>File 2 consists of the following document:</u>

[A] GENERAL POWER OF ATTORNEY

BY SAMANTHA S. SMITH	UNITED STATES OF AMERICA
IN FAVOR OF JODI HATCH	STATE OF LOUISIANA
OR LORI HATCH	PARISH OF WASHINGTON

BE IT KNOWN that on November 5, 2020, before me, Yvette Townswend, a notary public duly qualified in and for the above stated state and parish, and in the presence of the named and undersigned competent witnesses, personally appeared SAMANTHA S. SMITH, a person over the age of majority and a domiciliary of Caddo Parish, Louisiana, who declared under oath that she has been married once to Joseph Earl, Jr., from whom she is widowed, and has not since remarried, and whose mailing address is 1008 Jones Avenue, Apt. 3, Shreveport, LA 71105, and who declared that she appoints Jodi Hatch and Lori Hatch as independent agents, each being able to act independently without consultation of the other to perform the acts authorized in this power of attorney, hereinafter referred to as "agent" or "agents," to be her agent, representative, and attorney-in-fact, with full power and authority to act for, in the name of and on behalf of principal, to do all acts necessary or deemed by agent to be appropriate to represent principal including, but not limited to, the following:

1. Business and Affairs. To conduct, manage, and transact the business and personal financial matters of principal, of every nature and kind without any exception, including the transfer, sale, mortgaging, or encumbrance of real estate owned by principal.

2. Loans. To borrow money in principal's name from any bank or other financial institution; to make, issue, and endorse any promissory note in the name of principal, and to renew the same from time to time; to deliver, pledge, and pawn the same.

3. General. To do and perform each and every other act, matter or thing as may

be appropriate in agent's discretion as if such act, matter or thing were or had been particularly stated in this instrument.

[B] THUS DONE AND PASSED, on the day, month, and year first above written, in the presence of the undersigned competent witnesses who have signed their names together with the principal and me, notary, in Bogalusa, Louisiana.

_____x_____
SAMANTHA S. SMITH, ___**[C]**___

_____x_____
Linda Earl

_____x_____
Frank Johnson

_____
Yvette Townsend, Notary Public
Notary ID no. 123456

The undersigned accepts the appointment created by this power of attorney to act as the principal's true and lawful agent, representative, and attorney-in-fact.

[D] _____x_____ date: _____ , 2021
Jodi Hatch

_____x_____ **[E]** date: _____ , 2021
Lori Hatch

7

Exam B

Number of questions: 36 | Time limit: 2 hours, 35 minutes

Section 1 • Testaments and Trusts

SCENARIO: While he was alive, Andy owned a house he bought with his wife Tess using funds they each earned at their jobs. The house is worth $200,000. He also had a fancy Ming vase he inherited from his brother, worth $10,000, and two years before he and Tess married he bought 20 shares of Apple stock that he has not touched or traded over the years (valued at $3000 at his death). Tess and Andy have one child, a daughter (age 19) named Dora. Andy has recently died. Andy's mother, Nana, is still alive, as are Tess and Dora.

1. Assume that Andy died leaving solely an appropriately drafted notarial testament (which, among other actions, named the notary to be executor). It was signed by Andy, witnessed and signed by Nana and Dora, then signed by the notary. The testament leaves all of Andy's estate to Dora. Which of the following statements is false?

A. Nana was a valid and competent witness to the testament despite her maternal relationship to Andy.

B. Andy may grant ownership of the entirety of his estate to Dora despite his marriage to Tess because his estate does not include Tess's share of the house.

C. The testament is invalid, and the court in the succession will not accept the appointment of the notary as the executor, because Dora is a legatee.

D. Dora was not a competent witness to the testament, but in the succession, Dora will receive the entirety of Andy's estate.

2. In the situation immediately above, assuming Dora and Nana are valid and proper witnesses to the testament, which of the following statements is true?

A. The notary may not serve as executor of the testament because the notary cannot be both notary and legatee to a testament, thereby invalidating the will.

B. The notary may not serve as executor of the testament because a notary is by definition also an official witness to the act; witnesses are prohibited by law from serving as executor.

C. The notary may not serve as executor of the testament because the notary cannot be both notary and legatee to a testament, thereby invalidating that assignment of executor but not invalidating the rest of the will.

D. The testament is not invalid for naming the notary as executor, and the notary may serve as executor, because the designation of an executor is not a legacy.

3. Assume for this question only that the testament, which is otherwise complete and valid, leaves most of Andy's estate to Dora but also leaves one-eighth of it to any other child that may be born to him within five months of his death. In fact Andy has an additional child, Bob, born to him posthumously, a month after he died. At the time of the succession, Bob is six months old. Which of the following statements is false?

A. Because Bob was in utero at the time of Andy's death, Bob is a proper legatee and has capacity to receive a donation mortis causa.

B. Bob's legacy will consist of one-quarter of Andy's estate, not the one-eighth stated in the testament.

C. Bob has capacity to receive property under the will even if he was a test-tube baby but, as a fertilized ovum, was not implanted until after Andy's death.

D. If Andy had no testament at his death, Bob would have the capacity to receive property absent the will even if he was a test-tube baby but, as a fertilized ovum, was not implanted until after Andy's death.

4. Assume for this question that the testament leaves most of the estate to Andy's child or children but also grants ownership of his Ming vase to the Caddo Museum of Art, a nonprofit art collection. The disposition of the vase is an example of:

A. A universal legacy.

B. A particular legacy.

C. A charitable trust.

D. A general legacy.

5. To establish the donation of the vase in the preceding example, Andy has stated in his testament: "I would like that the Ming vase my brother gave to me be given to the Caddo Museum of Art, whose address, Executive Director, and other contact information are found on a brochure in my office desk drawer." Which of the following statements is true?

A. The incorporation of additional documents to a testament is forbidden and so the legacy to the museum will fail.

B. The testamentary donation to the museum will not be enforced unless the testament is placed in the will registry maintained by the Louisiana Secretary of State, and it is the primary duty of the notary to so record it.

C. In the testament, Andy has validly bequeathed the vase to the museum, and the court in the succession is likely to enforce Andy's stated direction over the objection of Dora.

D. The grant of the vase to the museum is not likely to be considered binding at law since the words are precatory.

6. Assume the grant of the vase in the preceding two questions. But now, Andy's testament provides that the vase at his death will be granted to the Caddo Museum of Art but that, should the museum decline to accept it, the vase would be granted to the Bossier Museum of Art. The Caddo museum rejects the donation, but the Bossier museum would be willing to accept it. May it do so?

A. Yes, because this is a permitted form of vulgar substitution.

B. No, because substitutions are forbidden, and the testament purports to have the Bossier museum substitute for the Caddo one in the event the legacy lapses.

C. Yes, because all substitutions of legatees are allowed in an otherwise valid testament, to promote the general policy against having legacies lapse.

D. No, because once a legacy is inherited by one party it becomes theirs in naked ownership, such that it is not the proper role of the testator to give it to another party.

7. In the original scenario, assume that Andy left a valid will which properly included a clause naming Nana as executrix. As executrix to the succession, Nana is told she must put up collateral in lieu of a bond to serve as representative. This is considered to be:

A. A conventional mortgage.

B. A legal mortgage.

C. A pledge.

D. A judicial mortgage.

For the following questions related to this scenario, use the original scenario and assume the following additional statement of fact: Andy's only written testament, above, is not valid and would be considered null by any measure. The Apple stock did not gain in value and paid no dividends during the marriage.

8. Assume Andy's testament is not valid. Dora, without good reason, has not communicated with Andy for three years before his death. Dora's occupation is a full-time clerk at Walmart. Which of the following statements is true?

A. In the succession, the court will consider Dora to be a forced heir because the lack of communication only lasted a year after she became 18.

B. In the succession, the court will not consider Dora to be a forced heir if she failed to communicate with Andy for three years without just cause.

C. In the succession, the existence of forced heirship by Dora is considered to be irrelevant under the circumstances.

D. In the succession, the existence of forced heirship by Dora will be denied by the court because she is an unworthy successor.

9. Assume the will is invalid and in any event was silent as to disinherison. Who will inherit the house?

A. Half of the house will go to Dora and the other half is owned by Tess. Tess has a usufruct in the house which ends when she dies or remarries.

B. The house goes to Dora, and Tess has a usufruct in the house which ends when she dies or remarries.

C. The house goes to Tess, and Dora has a usufruct in the house which ends when Tess dies or remarries, at which time Dora will gain full ownership of the house.

D. The house goes to Dora who will own it. Usufruct for Tess would only apply if the will had been found to be valid.

10. What is the *gross* value of Andy's estate at the time he died?

A. $115,000

B. $113,000

C. $213,000

D. $108,000

11. Assume that Dora, Tess, and Nana wish to avoid a judicial proceeding to sort out the estate and make clear that they own the things they legally inherit. A method of doing so is:

A. not available in this instance because the house was community property

B. available and found in the Louisiana Civil Code book titled "Persons"

C. available and found in the Louisiana Code of Civil Procedure

D. not available in this instance because of the value of the estate, such that the notary should instead prepare succession papers for the legatees

12. Assume that Tess and Nana died before Andy, and that Dora has no relatives. If she wishes to have the notary receive a "small succession" form, which of the following statements is false?

A. The document must declare that Andy died intestate.

B. Two witnesses must witness Dora sign the document, and then the notary signs.

C. The document must be signed by Dora and a witness with knowledge of the factual circumstances of the property and family, such as that Dora has no relatives, and then the notary signs.

D. The document must contain a listing of each piece of property and its value, in addition to the total value of the estate.

For the remaining questions related to this scenario, use the original scenario and assume the following additional statement of fact: Andy's only written testament, above, is valid.

13. Assume now that Andy also owned a Rolex watch worth $2000 which he had received as a gift at his college graduation, before he met Tess. In the original testament (now seen as otherwise valid), the testator added a clause in which "he devises the Rolex watch to Sue to hold in trust for Dora until she turns 25." For this transaction, Andy is considered to be:

A. naked owner

B. principal beneficiary

C. trustee

D. settlor

14. For this preceding transaction, Sue is considered to be:

A. naked owner

B. principal beneficiary

C. trustee

D. settlor

15. If this trust was instead established inter vivos, and Andy named himself as trustee, would the transaction be proper?

A. No, because a donor is not allowed to reserve a usufruct to himself while donating ownership of a thing.

B. Yes, because a donor is allowed to reserve a usufruct to himself if the thing is considered to be a movable, like a watch, whereas the answer is much more unclear if the thing is an immovable.

C. Yes, because the settlor of a trust made during the life of the original owner may also serve as trustee.

D. No, because the settlor of a trust is dispossessed of ownership once the trust is established, whereas the trustee is the true owner of a thing.

16. Assume now that Andy wishes to create a trust naming Sue as trustee and Dora as beneficiary of the watch. By which process may he set up this trust?

A. By a valid testament, whether notarial or olographic.

B. By a document prepared in authentic form but not by a private or acknowledged act.

C. By a document prepared in authentic form or by one created by a private act in front of two witnesses then duly acknowledged by one of the witnesses before a notary.

D. Both A and B would legally accomplish the goal he intends.

E. Both A and C would legally accomplish the goal he intends.

17. Assume instead that the watch is granted inter vivos in trust to the accounting firm of Ace & Barrow (a partnership) for the benefit of the nonprofit corporation Watches Remembrance. Is this allowed?

A. Yes, because a beneficiary, trust, and trustee may be juridical persons, which is permitted here because the settlor is a natural person.

B. Yes, because a beneficiary and trustee may be juridical persons, which is permitted here whether or not the settlor is a natural person.

C. Yes, because a beneficiary and trustee may be juridical persons, which is permitted here because the settlor is a natural person.

D. No, because although a charitable trust allows the beneficiary of a trust to be a nonprofit corporation, the trustee who actually owns the property must be a natural person.

18. For the preceding trust established inter vivos by Andy in which Ace & Barrow would own the property for the benefit of Watches Remembrance, assume the parties have the capacity to act in the roles assigned to them by the trust instrument. Watches Remembrance (WR) wishes to decline the gift of the watch. Valid proof that WR has done so is that:

A. WR refuses the watch by an authentic act.

B. WR refuses the watch in writing.

C. WR refuses to take possession of the watch.

D. Both A and B are valid methods of establishing the decision.

19. Assume the trust instrument in the preceding question has Ace & Barrow accept the watch for the benefit of Dora but that all revenues from the watch (such as fees from displaying it in commercials) go to Nana. Which of the following statements is true?

A. Ace & Barrow have the authority to tap into the commercial fees to make sure that Dora's educational, medical, or similar needs are met.

B. Dora receives no benefit from the watch until Nana dies, after which ownership becomes perfect in Dora.

C. Dora is the true owner of the watch while Nana is the beneficiary.

D. Dora and Nana are considered to be successive income beneficiaries.

20. Andy decides that he would like his body to be cremated at his death. He thinks a friend named Janet is more likely to honor that request than some of his relatives. How may he accomplish this designation in a way that is binding on Tess and his legatees?

A. appropriate designation of Janet in an olographic testament

B. notarized document setting forth his designation of Janet to handle his body

C. appropriate designation of Janet in a notarial testament

D. all of the above accomplish this goal

E. both B and C accomplish this goal

Section 2 • Power of Attorney

*Using the document shown as **File 2** in our Library (General Power of Attorney), answer the following questions.*

21. Assuming the document is completed and signed as indicated, line A of the document would instead appropriately read:

A. Medical Power of Attorney

B. Mandate

C. Authorization of Legal Representation

D. Procuration

22. What word likely appears on line C?

A. Principal

B. Affiant

C. Mandatary

D. Trustee

23. Linda Earl is 14 years old but appears to be mature and knowledgeable about Samantha's need for a power of attorney. Linda is the daughter of Samantha Smith. Is Linda prohibited from serving in this role?

A. No, neither her age nor her relationship with Samantha disqualifies her.

B. Her age disqualifies her but her relationship with Samantha does not disqualify her.

C. Yes, her age and her relationship with Samantha disqualify her.

D. Her age does not disqualify her but her relationship with Samantha does disqualify her.

24. As to other legal issues or concerns fairly presented by this file document, which of the following is a problem?

A. The venue clause should simply be the state and parish of signing, rather than information about the parties involved and the country.

B. The appearance clause should include a declaration of change in marital status.

C. There should not be witness lines and signatures if this document is used to merely authorize Jodi or Lori to lease an apartment on behalf of Samantha.

D. Only one agent should be appointed as the primary representative of Samantha.

E. None of the above is a concern or issue with this document, given its stated purpose.

25. Assume that there are no witnesses when this document is signed by Samantha. Jodi will later use this document to donate a plot of land that Samantha owns to Clyde, with no compensation paid by Clyde and no conditions placed on the gift. The transaction will be prohibited because:

A. A general power of attorney must be an authentic act.

B. The power of attorney in this situation must be in authentic form.

C. Clyde is not named in the given instrument.

D. There is no property description of the plot of land in the given instrument.

26. In the preceding question, which of the following details in the instrument would make it invalid to accomplish the intended purpose?

A. The clause in paragraph B is incomplete.

B. It is signed in Washington Parish but the appearance clause states that Samantha has her domicile in Caddo Parish.

C. The date on line E is November 22, 2020.

D. The clause in paragraph 1 does not specify the type of conveyance which Jodi is attempting to accomplish.

27. In the previous question, focusing on the appearance clause, assume now that Samantha and Linda have a home at the Shreveport address listed, in Caddo Parish. Caddo is not properly described as the appearer's domicile if, at the time of signing:

A. Samantha and Linda live in an apartment in Bossier Parish while the Shreveport home is undergoing extensive renovations.

B. Two days before, Samantha voted in Bossier Parish.

C. Linda lives separately with a grandmother in Washington Parish.

D. Samantha currently lives in a long-term rehabilitation center in Washington Parish, because she was injured in a serious accident on October 25, 2020, and will continue to do so for the foreseeable future.

28. Assume for this question that Linda and Frank signed their lines when Lori and Jodi did, a day after Samantha executed the instrument, which is nonetheless valid. Which of the following acts that it specifically authorizes can validly be accomplished by Lori, using this document as the basis for her authority?

A. designation of tutor for Linda

B. statement of authority for an unincorporated association Samantha owns

C. credit sale of a mobile home that Samantha owns

D. concurrence to the adoption of Linda when she reaches 18

29. Assume the original document is completed as written and signed on November 5 by everyone named. Assume it includes a provision expressly authorizing the representative to do several specific acts regarding the house in Shreveport that Samantha owns. Which of the following may not be done by Jodi?

A. establish a right of passage in favor of the neighboring plot of land

B. enter into a settlement of a dispute with a neighbor over the location of hedges

C. establish a servitude of light in favor of the neighboring home's bedroom window

D. all of the above may be done by Jodi with express authority

E. none of the above may be done by Jodi even with express authority

30. Jodi enters into a sales contract with a furniture store for the purchase of a sofa, having disclosed to the store that she is serving as an agent for someone in this matter but without naming Samantha in particular. Jodi fails to perform under the terms of the contract. Is Jodi liable for this failure?

A. No, because she is acting on behalf of Samantha, within the limits of her authority.

B. Yes, because the store has fulfilled its duty to determine the name of the principal.

C. No, because the store is aware that this is an agency arrangement and cannot reasonably expect the representative to pay.

D. Yes, because Samantha's identity was unknown to the store when she made the contract.

31. Even if paragraphs 1–3 of the instrument specify the authority in detail, the power of attorney may not be used to:

A. Execute a testament on behalf of the principal testator.

B. Execute an affidavit on behalf of the principal affiant.

C. Make a donation of an immovable owned by the principal.

D. All of the above are correct.

E. Both A and B are correct.

32. Assume the original document was correctly drafted and executed, but that Jodi is the only named representative (Lori is not mentioned). Jodi is using it to authorize her supervision of renovations on the Shreveport home. Assuming the authorization has not been otherwise revoked, if Samantha dies:

A. The authority automatically and fully terminates once both Samantha and Jodi have died.

B. The authority automatically and fully terminates at Samantha's death.

C. The authority continues for actions begun by Jodi before Samantha died, in order to protect Samantha's property or preserve her estate.

D. The authority continues until an executor is named such that Samantha's affairs can be taken over by the executor.

33. In the preceding question, while Jodi was supervising the renovations but before Samantha died, Jodi needed to take out a mortgage on the house to complete the project. In the mortgage's appearance clause, where Jodi appears, the clause:

A. should list Samantha first, then Jodi

B. is required to provide only Samantha's name and information

C. should list Jodi first, then Samantha

D. is required to provide only Jodi's name and information

34. In the preceding situation, assume that Jodi is the one to sign the mortgage. All of the following are acceptable ways for her to fill in the signature line except:

A. cursive writing that says Samantha S. Smith

B. cursive writing that says Jodi Hatch

C. block letters that read JODI HATCH

D. a squiggle that one can reasonably make out as reading JHatch

35. Assume the original document in the library was completed as written, and signed on November 5 by everyone named. A year later, Samantha suffers a stroke and no longer has the capacity to deal with her financial and property management matters. Which of the following is true?

A. A statement by medical doctors establishing Samantha's incapacity must be executed in authentic form.

B. The power of attorney continues in force and allows Jodi to perform the acts it authorizes.

C. The power of attorney is terminated by Samantha's condition unless it originally included a clause declaring it to be durable.

D. The representative must have the incapacity of Samantha established by a notarized act by herself and an attending physician.

36. Jodi and Lori decide to form a Louisiana corporation. They want to name it Bons Temps Rouler Co. Is that a permitted name?

A. No, because it is not in the English language.

B. Yes, assuming it is their trade name registered with the Secretary of State.

C. No, because it should end in "Corp." or "Inc."

D. Yes, because it uses English characters.

STOP. END EXAM B.

8

Library Document for Exam C

This is the library to refer to, for some of the questions in Exam C. In all libraries, a line with an x on it is actually signed there. The x is not just a place where the signature goes; consider it to be signed.

<u>File 3 consists of the following document:</u>

STATE OF LOUISIANA

PARISH OF ST. MARY

LAST WILL AND TESTAMENT

BEFORE ME came Sandra Sheeren, a resident of 123 Manson St., Franklin, LA, who after being duly sworn deposes and says:

1. She has full capacity to make this will and testament and has no children.

2. She wishes to dispose of her property at death. She owns 40 shares of GiantCo common stock, 10 gold coins, her residence at 123 Manson St., Franklin, LA, and a 2012 motorcycle.

3. She prefers that the stock and coins go to her nephew Ed Sheeren, and the residence and bike go to her friend Gary Green, who also lives in Franklin.

4. This notarized testament revokes and rescinds her testament of Dec. 11, 2016.

Sworn to and subscribed before me this 2nd day of May, 2020, in Lake Charles, Louisiana.

_____x_____
Sandra Sheeren, Testator

WITNESSES:

_____x_____   _____x_____
Tommy Thomas   Jan Jett

            _____x_____
                        T.J. Fazzio, Notary Public

9

Exam C

Number of questions: 39 | Time limit: 2 hours, 50 minutes

Section 1 • Donations

SCENARIO: The parties to an instrument (signed in St. Charles Parish) donating, from A to B, a tract of land located in both Livingston Parish and Ascension Parish instruct the notary to return the original to B so that B will record it in the appropriate parish or parishes. The instruction about recordation is stated in the instrument.

1. For the above executed instrument, which of the following statements is true?

A. The instrument with its express direction of delivery to B relieves the notary of the statutory duty of recordation, assuming the notary gave the original, executed document to B.

B. The instrument must be recorded by the notary within 48 hours of its execution, because it is a statutory duty of the notary to file documents relating to immovables.

C. The instrument must be recorded by the notary within 15 days of its execution, because it is a statutory duty of the notary to file documents relating to immovables.

D. The instrument with its express direction allows the notary to fulfill the statutory duty of recordation by ascertaining within 15 days that B has registered the document appropriately.

2. In the above scenario, assume for this question only that the act was not a donation, but rather the request for cancellation of a mortgage originally made by A for the benefit of B. Which of the following statements is true?

A. If a bank is requesting the cancellation, it must be executed or acknowledged in front of a notary.

B. The request must be accompanied by a document in authentic form describing the obligation, assuming the original mortgage was secured by a non-paraphed obligation.

C. The mortgagee has the duty to cancel the mortgage once the secured debt is satisfied.

D. The mortgagor has the duty to cancel the mortgage once the secured debt is satisfied; such a demand requires the signature of each party to the original mortgage.

E. None of the above statements is true.

3. Assume in the original scenario (involving a donation) that the notary fails to fulfill a statutory duty of recordation. What consequence(s) may apply to the notary?

A. The violation of a law governing the exercise of notarial authority may be considered "cause" for which a district court may suspend the notary.

B. The violation of a law governing the exercise of notarial authority may be considered an offense for which the notary may be automatically suspended by operation of law.

C. The violation of a law governing the exercise of notarial authority may be subject the notary to a fine of $200.

D. All of the above statements are true.

E. Both A and C are true.

4. Regardless of who files the above donation instrument for recordation, which of the following statements is true?

A. The original instrument must be filed in Livingston Parish.

B. The original instrument must be filed in Ascension Parish.

C. The original instrument must be filed in St. Charles Parish.

D. The original instrument may be filed in Livingston Parish, where the clerk of court may issue a certified copy, and that copy is then filed in Ascension Parish.

E. The original instrument may be filed in Livingston Parish as long as the notary executes, from an exact photocopy, a Certified True Copy, which is then filed in Ascension Parish.

5. In the original scenario, assume for this question only that the party "A" is 17 years old and married to "C." His donation is to "B," who is his father. Which of the following statements is false?

A. The notary has the power to file the document even if she or he was commissioned before 2005 and only holds a commission in St. Charles Parish.

B. A doesn't have the capacity to donate the tract of land because he is a minor and the donation is not made to C.

C. A has the capacity to make this donation because he is an emancipated minor, due to being married.

D. A would be able to make this donation to his father but only in the form of a donation mortis causa.

6. In the above scenario, and for this question only, assume that the notary holds a commission (and lives in) St. Charles Parish, received in 1997 after taking and passing a parish-wide notary exam in which the applicant drafted various instruments. The notary has not since taken a state-wide exam. Now, the parties wish to have the document executed in Jefferson Parish. Which of the following statements is true?

A. The notary may do so if she or he has applied for and holds a concurrent commission in Jefferson Parish, as long as the notary maintains an office in Jefferson Parish and posts a separate surety bond for each parish.

B. The notary may do so because of the reciprocal jurisdiction afforded certain parish groups.

C. The notary may do so because Jefferson Parish is adjacent to St. Charles Parish, as long as the notary or the notary's employer has an office in Jefferson Parish.

D. The notary may do so if she or he has applied for and holds a concurrent commission in Jefferson Parish, as long as the notary maintains an office in Jefferson Parish, whether or not the notary posts a separate surety bond for each parish because the two parishes are adjoining.

E. Both B and D are true.

7. In the original instrument making the donation from A to B, assume that A wishes to make the transfer effective 14 days after the signing of the instrument, so he has time to move his personal items. A and B sign the instrument containing this express instruction. Is the donation valid?

A. Yes, assuming that B's part in signing it included a clear acceptance of a donation and not simply vague statements of receiving the property.

B. No, it is not a valid donation, because its effective date is delayed.

C. Yes, but it does not become effective until the 14 days mentioned in the instruction.

D. No, because the deadline for the filing date precludes the grace period added.

8. Assume the previous instrument is otherwise valid. Which of the following statements or declarations do NOT need to be included?

A. last four digits of B's social security number

B. legal property description of the tract of land

C. change in marital status of A

D. designation of who will pay the property taxes

9. Assume that A is not the naked owner of the property but holds a usufruct. Which of the following statements is true?

A. A may not donate inter vivos his usufructary interest to B, since it is a personal servitude.

B. A may donate inter vivos his usufructary interest to B even though it is a personal servitude.

C. A may donate inter vivos the tract of land along with his usufructary interest to B.

D. A may make a donation mortis causa of his usufructary interest to B.

Section 2 • Testaments and Successions

*Using the document shown as **File 3** in our Library (Last Will and Testament), answer the following questions.*

10. Which of the following attributes of the library document will NOT make Sandra's testament invalid or violate statutory requirements for such an act?

A. The conclusion is in the form of a jurat.

B. Parts of the will are written from the point of view of the notary public.

C. The notary's name is Tauseef Julio Fazzio.

D. The will ends without the notary adding his identification number.

11. A court may find Sandra's testament or a legacy in it to be invalid (or the notary to have failed to perform a required duty) because:

A. Juridical acts in the form of an affidavit never have witnesses sign too.

B. She ambiguously lists some property in paragraph 2 but may not be listing other important parts of her estate.

C. She revokes the December 11, 2016 will but ignores one she executed in 2018.

D. The house on Manson was acquired in 2017 during a marriage she has not mentioned here.

E. Her appearance clause does not state her parish of domicile, just residence.

12. Sandra reads the document, understands it, and signs it on the appropriate signature line. Jan Jett is 16 years old and deaf. Will this make the testament invalid?

A. No, but only if Jan is determined by the court to be relatively mature and fully understood the nature and consequences of the testator's act.

B. Yes, because, deaf people do not have the capacity to serve as a witness to a will.

C. No, because there is nothing to indicate that Jan is not competent to serve as witness under the circumstances.

D. Yes, because Jan had not reached the age of majority at the time the will was signed.

13. Assume that Tommy Thomas, age 33 and unrelated to Sandra, is named as executor in the will and also is designated specifically to receive a gold watch that Sandra owns. Will these provisions of the will make it invalid?

A. Yes, because being named as executor makes Tommy a legatee and as such he cannot serve as witness.

B. Yes, because being named as recipient of the watch makes Tommy a legatee and as such he cannot serve as witness.

C. No, but he will not be allowed to serve as executor.

D. No, but he cannot enforce the legacy of the gold watch.

E. Both A and B are correct.

14. Assume for this question that Tommy Thomas is unable to sign his name in full and wishes to place a mark on the blank instead to confirm he witnessed Sandra's will. May he do so (and the will remain valid)?

A. No, because juridical acts require that the signature match the full name of the witness.

B. Yes, because the mark may satisfy the requirement of a signature for a will, whether olographic or notarial.

C. No, because witnesses to notarial wills may not use a mark instead of a signature.

D. Yes, because witnesses to juridical acts may use a mark instead of a signature.

15. Assume for this question only that the testament is otherwise valid. It turns out that Sandra has no children but once had a son, and that son (since deceased, and he would've been 22 when Sandra died) had a boy named Hugh. No other children or grandchildren exist. Hugh is now 3. Assuming Sandra's entire estate has a gross value of 120,000, and no debts, which of the following statements is true?

A. Sandra's heirs are eligible to use the succession-by-affidavit procedure.

B. Despite being left out of the testament, Hugh will receive from the estate a value of $30,000.

C. Hugh can be validly left out of the succession, and not receive property from the estate, because only children are forced heirs.

D. Hugh will be treated as the only living successor in the first degree and will inherit everything.

16. Assume the present will is valid but that Gary Green has died before Sandra, himself leaving no successors. The residence on Manson Street is worth $123,000. Sandra has recently died but no succession has been opened; some in her family have decided that the motorcycle (worth $2000) should go, as soon as possible, to a friend named Stu rather than to Ed or another nephew named Craig. They may accomplish this result without opening a succession by using only:

A. Succession by affidavit.

B. Affidavit of heirship form.

C. Power of attorney.

D. None of the above by itself will accomplish this goal.

17. Sandra executed a valid will in 2013 in addition to the (otherwise valid) will of December 11, 2016. Assuming the present will is NOT valid, and Sandra dies, a court is likely to:

A. Enforce the 2013 will.

B. Find that Sandra died testate, leaving her property to the heirs named in a valid will.

C. Find that Sandra died intestate.

D. Enforce the 2016 will.

18. If the will is otherwise valid, is the court in a succession likely to enforce the legacy that says that "the stock and coins go to her nephew Ed Sheeren"?

A. No, because a stated preference is not a donation mortis causa.

B. No, because Ed is a nephew, not a legatee in the first degree.

C. Yes, because both incorporeal movables (stock) and corporeal movables (coins) may be validly included in the dispositive portion of a testament.

D. Yes, assuming their value is less than half of the estate.

19. Assume for this question that the will is valid and also that at the time it is signed Sandra is married to Keevin. The will appoints Keevin to be executor and bequeaths him a valuable tiara. Before Sandra dies, she divorces Keevin but doesn't change or revoke the will. In the succession, which statement is true?

A. Keevin will receive the tiara but not be appointed executor.

B. Keevin will not receive the tiara but will be appointed executor.

C. Keevin will not receive the tiara and not be appointed executor.

D. Keevin will receive the tiara and be appointed executor, despite being named Keevin.

20. For the original library document, assume the instrument is found to be invalid and there is no other such instrument. If Ed receives property anyway, it is because:

A. the succession is intestate and he is the heir

B. the succession is testate and he is the heir

C. the succession is intestate and he is the legatee

D. the succession is testate and he is the legatee

Section 3 • Affidavits

SCENARIO: A notary, Nancy, is asked to receive and verify an affidavit by her long-time friend John as part of John's ongoing divorce proceedings in Baton Rouge. John's attorney, who lives in St. Helena Parish but has an office in East Feliciana Parish, prepared the document and, most likely, will file it in East Baton Rouge Parish along with several court petitions. At the top of the form (as with the petitions), where the caption and court information is located, it states "State of Louisiana" but has a blank for Parish of _____" below that, and other spaces to the right of the state and parish for the case number and specific division of court. The document is signed and received in St. Martin Parish.

21. The notary should fill in the "parish of" blank as:

A. St. Martin Parish.

B. East Feliciana Parish.

C. East Baton Rouge Parish.

D. The notary should not fill in the blank.

22. In the preceding affidavit, the clause immediately below John's name and signature is:

A. evidence of oath

B. attestation clause

C. jurat

D. paraph

23. For this question, assume that the document is a declaration to establish that a mobile home on a farm John owns in another parish is henceforth a component part of the farm. Nancy plans to make the document in the form of an affidavit, signed by John and herself without witnesses. Will it be valid?

A. Yes, because such an act or declaration must be in affidavit form.

B. No, because such an act or declaration must be in authentic form.

C. Yes, because such an act or declaration need not be witnessed by more than the notary herself.

D. No, because such an act or declaration must be an authentic act or an act under private signature duly acknowledged with witnesses.

24. Nancy passed the state notary exam in 2011 and lives only in Cameron Parish, which is nowhere near St. Martin Parish. Nonetheless, as a favor for her old friend John, while on a trip through St. Martin Parish, she stops there long enough to receive and verify the affidavit after watching John sign it. It is a straightforward affidavit setting forth facts about his divorce and finances. Nancy did not bring along her rubber stamp or embosser. Nonetheless she signs the signature line for the notary and writes her name and notary identification number immediately below that. Is the way she has endorsed the document sufficient?

A. Yes, because it is John's signature that makes the document a declaration under oath with the penalty of perjury, and thus a valid affidavit in Louisiana.

B. No, because for the most official purposes, such as a court filing, the notary should use the rubber stamp and mark from an embosser somewhere below the signature line.

C. Yes, because a Louisiana court would recognize that a Louisiana notary's signature is her seal.

D. No, because although she may administer an oath in any jurisdiction, she is not eligible to notarize an act or affidavit in St. Martin Parish.

25. In the preceding example, Nancy forgot to ask John to see his drivers' license. Is the affidavit valid?

A. Yes, because John is personally known to her.

B. Yes, assuming she has verified his identity from another acceptable proof of identification such as John's U.S. passport or military ID.

C. No, because notaries follow a strict rule of personal identification and must see a state-issued drivers' license or identification card.

D. Yes, assuming he is a student in a state-licensed college or university and presented his official student ID card.

26. In the preceding example, John also introduces Nancy to Frankie, a witness to certain facts relevant to the divorce. The attorney has prepared an affidavit for Frankie's signature. Nancy uses proper procedure in receiving the affidavit, including watching Frankie sign it and then placing her seal on it as well. But she has not seen any identification from Frankie. John has known Frankie since college. Is the affidavit valid?

A. Yes, because one signator to a legal instrument or instruments may verify and vouch for the identity of another signator, as long as the one so vouching is properly identified through a statutorily acceptable form of notary identification such as a state drivers' license.

B. Yes, because one signator to a legal instrument or instruments may verify and vouch for the identity of another signator, as long as the one so vouching is properly identified through a federally-issued identification such as a U.S. Passport or military ID.

C. Yes, because John is personally known to her, assuming he vouches for the identity of Frankie.

D. No, because in this instance they are not signing one document together, such as a lease, but instead the affidavits are two separate instruments.

27. Frankie asserts in his affidavit (among many other facts) that John owns a 2016 Nissan Sentra car. Nancy noticed that John apparently has a new red Mercedes outside. May she receive and verify the affidavit of Frankie without more information or discussion?

A. No, because the notary's independent duty of establishing capacity requires her to inquire further into who owns the red Mercedes and why it is not mentioned in this document.

B. Yes, because an affidavit is personal to the affiant and is not something that can be signed by anyone else for him or her.

C. No, because formal juridical acts including testaments require that the notary review the dispositive portions with the appearer(s) and verify that they understand the import of those portions.

D. Yes, because the notary signing an affidavit is verifying that an oath was administered and that the one appearing swears to the facts he or she asserts; the notary is not verifying the truth of the contents stated in the affidavit itself.

28. John also has an affidavit with him that is signed and dated (today) by Frankie's spouse Terry. Terry is ill at home. Terry is well known by John, who himself is well known by Nancy. John recognizes Terry's signature and assures Nancy that it is Terry's. Which of the following statements is true?

A. This is not sufficient to identify Terry unless Frankie has also brought along Terry's drivers' license or other statutorily required ID.

B. This is not sufficient to allow Nancy to verify Terry's signature.

C. This is sufficient to identify Terry because Nancy knows John well, and John knows Terry well and so vouches for her identity.

D. This may make the affidavit valid if Terry signed it in front of Frankie as a witness, and Frankie executes a witness acknowledgment with Nancy.

Section 4 • Property Descriptions and Conveyances

29. Review the following incomplete but otherwise correct portion of a statement incorporated into an instrument transferring ownership of a farm. (The plaque mentioned is one commemorating the founding of Townville.)

… more particularly described as follows: commencing at the NE corner of the SE 1/4 of Sec 4, T5S, R8W, proceed S 140 ft to a set commemorative plaque, being the point of beginning, thence S 2640 ft, thence W 1320 ft, thence N 1320 ft, thence E 660 ft, thence N 1320 ft, thence E 660 ft to the _____ , …

The above statement is an example of:

A. per aversionem

B. metes and bounds

C. section of township

D. subdivision plat

30. In the preceding partial statement, the marker commemorating the founding of Townville is understood to be:

A. point of beginning

B. original bearing

C. commencing point

D. both A and C are correct

31. In the preceding statement, considering the blank line and the rest of the statement, which of the following is false?

A. The content of the blank line determines whether the description "closes the land."

B. If the blank line says "point of commencement," the description is flawed.

C. This property encompasses Section 4, Township 5 south, Range 8 west.

D. After the blank line is filled in correctly, the statement then continues, "…together with any and all improvements situated thereon."

32. Consider the following statement:

LOT 21. BLOCK 2. NEW CITY BLOCK 17326. THE GARDENS OF MOSSY OAKS SUBD. PLANNED UNIT DEVT. IN THE CITY OF MORGAN CITY, LOUISIANA ACCORDING TO PLAT THEREOF RECORDED IN VOL 9307 PAGES 155-158, DEED AND PLAT RECORDS OF ST MARY PARISH.

The statement is an example of:

A. part of a subdivision

B. closing the land

C. per aversionem

D. metes and bounds

33. In the above statement, because of what is missing from the typical one of this kind, the transaction involving the statement may be understood to involve:

A. a conventional mortgage

B. a donation of property not made as an authentic act

C. conveyance of the entire subdivision

D. sale of the land without the house that sits on it

34. Assume that the statement in the preceding question is not printed within the legal instrument itself but instead is found in a separate document. The legal instrument refers to the document for its contents but does not include the statement itself. The part of the instrument which refers to the separate document (which itself then contains the statement above) may be an example of a(n):

A. unincorporated association

B. jurat

C. recitation of paraph

D. act of incorporation

Section 5 • Forming a Limited Liability Company

SCENARIO: John, 17, is single and lives with his only parent, Susan, in Acadia Parish. She decides to give him the ability to sign contracts and form an LLC in his own name so that he can start a laptop-repair service.

35. What notarial instrument may validly accomplish this goal?

A. power of attorney

B. provisional custody by mandate

C. limited emancipation

D. adult adoption

36. In the instrument, assume that there were no witnesses at its execution. May the instrument still accomplish the desired goals mentioned in the scenario?

A. No, because without the witnesses it is not valid to allow John to perform any action for which he must be of the age of majority.

B. Yes, because it need not have witnesses since the actions of forming an LLC and signing contracts themselves don't need to be done in authentic form.

C. No, because without the witnesses it is not valid to perform the act of setting up an LLC which itself must be done in authentic form.

D. Yes, because it need not be in authentic form to authorize John to do any action for which he must be of the age of majority.

37. Assume the instrument is valid. Susan later writes a revision of the instrument that additionally adds a clause allowing John the power to write and execute a will, and to buy a car from Greg. Which of the following statements is false?

A. Emancipations are limited to the specific juridical acts enumerated in the instrument or otherwise provided by law.

B. John has the legal capacity to write a testament at his age, assuming he is capable of generally understanding the nature and consequences of the act.

C. Powers of attorney and mandates may not be used to empower someone to write a testament.

D. John is not allowed to write a valid testament until he is 18, whether or not this instrument is otherwise express and valid.

38. Assume in the previous question that the instrument is valid, as is the addition. John and Susan wish to have any bill of sale with Greg for the car transfer to be binding on Greg. For this to occur, they:

A. must file the modification in the same place they filed the original act: Acadia Parish.

B. must file the modification in Acadia Parish, but they need not have filed the original act.

C. need not file for registry either document.

D. must file for registry the original act (in Acadia Parish) but need only provide the original modification to Greg.

39. Susan is worried that any error John makes in his services could expose her to liability. In the original act, she inserts a clause that makes clear she is not responsible for errors and omissions he may make. Is she protected from such a concern?

A. Yes, because the instrument formed an LLC, which has the goal of making it difficult to reach personal assets.

B. Yes, because the clause she inserts into the instrument expressly waives liability.

C. No, because even an express waiver of liability in such an instrument will not have the effect she intends.

D. No, assuming she has not filed the instrument in the registry of the appropriate parish, because that is what makes it effective against third parties.

STOP. END EXAM C.

10

Mini-Exam D

Number of questions: 18 | Time limit: 1 hours, 20 minutes

Section 1 • Motor Vehicle Transactions

1. Roy is obtaining a new certificate of title on a 2009 Honda Civic which he just bought from Sam; they live near each other in Lafayette. Roy goes by Roy B. O'Hair, Sr. because his son is Roy, Jr.; it is important to keep himself and his son identifiable and thus he prefers to include the suffix as part of his name. What name will OMV use to issue a certificate of title to him?

A. ROY B OHAIR

B. ROY B OHAIR SR

C. ROY B. O'HAIR

D. ROY B. O'HAIR, SR.

2. In the preceding situation, which of the following was not a proper way for Sam to sign over the original certificate of title to Roy Sr.?

A. Sam signs the certificate of title on its back, in the presence of a notary, who signs it in the appropriate place on the back as well.

B. Sam and Roy sign the certificate of title on its back, both in the presence of a notary, who signs it in the appropriate place on the back as well.

C. Sam signs the certificate of title on its back, delivers it personally to Roy, who then signs it on the back in the presence of a notary, who signs it in the appropriate place on the back as well.

D. Sam signs the certificate of title on its back, in the presence of two witnesses who themselves sign the back of the title; one of the witnesses then executes an Acknowledgment of Witness before a notary, who signs the Acknowledgment in the appropriate place as well.

3. In the preceding transaction, in addition to the completed original certificate of title, which of the following is required to effectively assign title to Roy?

A. Disclosure of odometer mileage.

B. Bill of sale.

C. Power of attorney.

D. Both A and B, but not C, are required.

E. None of the above is required.

4. Assume for the question that Sam is donating, rather than selling, the car to Roy. Which of the following statements is false?

A. It is a valid donation even if not made by authentic act, and Roy acquires ownership of the car, if the donation is accompanied by actual delivery of the car to Roy and his acceptance by possession of it.

B. It is a valid donation but the State of Louisiana will require a written and authentic act of donation, written acceptance, and endorses title in order to issue a certificate of title in Roy's name.

C. It is a valid donation even without delivery to Roy and possession by Roy, if the donation is a writing done as an authentic act and Roy has written a clear acceptance of the car as a donation.

D. It is not a valid donation, and Roy does not own the car, unless the transfer is done by an authentic act of Sam and written acceptance by Roy, except if the donation is considered remunerative or onerous.

5. Roy is married to Tina, and they have a community property regime. Assume that Sam has donated the car only to Roy. Six weeks after he obtains title in his name, Roy, on his own volition and without compensation or expectation of benefit, decides that the Honda should be part of the community. How might this happen?

A. He would have to ask the OMV to reissue the title in both their names.

B. It is already part of the community even though title is in his name, and Tina owns an interest in half the car.

C. He can deliver the car to Tina and allow her to possess it, as a manual gift with no need to execute an authentic act.

D. He can transfer the car as separate property into the community by an authentic act.

Section 2 • Donations and Property

SCENARIO: Amy and Bart are married and own a condo, where they live in East Baton Rouge Parish, that they bought together a year after they married (they were married also while living in East Baton Rouge Parish). Two years later, they decide to sell the condo. Amy has to travel for business and may not be present at the time of the sale. They want Bart to be able to handle the act of sale without Amy's presence.

6. All of the following acts or instruments would accomplish the stated goal except:

A. procuration

B. declaration of acquisition of separate property

C. renunciation of right to concur

D. mandate

7. Inside the condo is a reclining chair worth little compared to the amount of money either Bart or Amy earns. Bart wants to donate the chair to his mother for Mother's Day. He does so without seeking approval of Amy, and the mother picks up the chair and starts to use it in her own home. Is there a legal problem with this transfer in that Amy did not approve of it in advance?

A. No, because both spouses need not agree to alienate movables such as furniture, only immovable property such as the condo.

B. Yes, the transfer failed at its inception, but because it is a relative nullity, the court will not declare the transaction invalid unless Amy objects.

C. Yes, the transfer failed at its inception, and as an absolute nullity, the transfer is invalid.

D. No, because both members of the community need not agree to the donation of furniture to a third party as long as the gift is of small value compared to the economic position of the spouses.

8. Was the previous donation, assuming it is otherwise valid for Bart to do unilaterally, properly done without using an authentic act?

A. Yes, because the mother has taken delivery of a corporal movable.

B. No, because the donation is neither onerous nor remunerative, assuming the mother is not paying any compensation for it nor has any conditions imposed upon her for its future use.

C. Yes, because the gift of certain incorporeal movables need not be made in authentic form as long there is compliance with the usual requirements applicable to the transfer of this particular kind of incorporeal movable.

D. No, because it is considered to be a donation in disguise.

9. Amy also owns a house in Jefferson Parish she bought on her own before they married. They will live in it when the condo sale closes, and she decides to transfer her interest in the house to make it become part of their legal regime. To validly do this:

A. Amy and Bart must appear before a notary and execute a transfer of the interest in a juridical act.

B. Amy must transfer her interest in the house by executing an authentic act, assuming she is placing no conditions on the transfer or is doing it out of the goodness of her heart.

C. Amy must transfer her interest in the house in writing.

D. Amy and Bart must appear before a notary and execute a transfer of the interest in an authentic act.

10. Assume for this question that the Jefferson Parish house was the separate property of Amy, as was her personal jewelry and clothing, because she and Bart had previously signed a valid prenuptial agreement removing themselves from the legal regime. To be effective towards third parties, the executed agreement must be:

A. Filed in the conveyance records of East Baton Rouge Parish.

B. Filed with the Office of Vital Records of the Louisiana Department of Health, in Baton Rouge.

C. Filed in the conveyance records of Jefferson Parish.

D. Filed in the conveyance records of East Baton Rouge Parish and Jefferson Parish.

11. The preceding agreement, to be valid at the time that the couple signs it, must be executed in the form of:

A. an authentic act or a private act duly acknowledged

B. an authentic act

C. a notarized agreement signed by both spouses

D. an affidavit signed by both spouses before a notary

Section 3 • Conveyances

SCENARIO: John sells his house to Helen by transferring ownership of the house in one instrument that also finances the purchase by establishing that the full cash price plus interest at 3% will be paid by Helen to John in monthly installments over ten years.

12. The form of transfer is:

A. act of sale with mortgage

B. sale with right of redemption

C. act of sale with vendor's privilege

D. act of cash sale

13. In the preceding transaction, assume that the instrument has a confession of judgment clause to allow John, in the event of Helen's default, to use executory process to retake the house. The instrument must include all the following except:

A. due-on-sale clause in favor of John

B. last four digits of Helen's social security number

C. two witness signatures to have the instrument be executed in authentic form

D. full legal description of the property, in addition to the municipal address

E. declaration of John's change in marital status since he acquired it

14. In the above transaction, eight years after it was properly completed, Helen finds that she in unable to keep up with the payments but does not want John to retake the home with the above process as she would still owe 20% of the original balance. They agree that she can return the house to John in a conveyance by which John forgives the remaining balance owed. This new conveyance is:

A. bond-for-deed

B. credit sale

C. dation en paiement

D. vente à réméré

E. quitclaim deed

15. In the original transaction when Helen first moved into the house, assume now that John and Helen instead agree that Helen will live there for five years, making payments each month until a set amount is reached, at which point John will deliver the title to Helen. This is known as:

A. bond-for-deed

B. credit sale

C. dation en paiement

D. vente à réméré

16. In the preceding transaction, at the time of the original agreement setting out the arrangement and payments, is there a requirement that the instrument be recorded?

A. Yes, because it is a conveyance of an immovable, which requires filing to be legally binding on both parties.

B. No, unless the parties wish to make sure that the arrangement legally affects third parties.

C. Yes, because even though the property is not conveyed at that time, its terms are not legally binding on both parties if it is not filed for registry.

D. No, because this form of arrangement does not culminate in the transfer of immovable property.

17. A legal description of a property, and not just a municipal address, is required by law to be included in all of the following except:

A. donation

B. act of sale

C. notarial testament

D. sale with right of redemption

18. Bill, married to Jane, writes an instrument that attempts to accomplish a donation mortis causa of his entire estate to his only child, Linda (who is 22 and not related to Jane). It is drafted properly by the notary and executed by Bill, two witnesses, and the notary. Is this donation permitted?

A. No, because there is a general prohibition against donating one's entire estate.

B. Yes, because this is an appropriate instance to allow donation of everything to Linda.

C. No, because of the law of forced heirship in which only part of his estate is the disposable portion.

D. Yes, assuming he has reserved a usufruct to Jane.

STOP. END EXAM D.

ANSWERS
AND
EXPLANATIONS

11

Answers and Explanations: Exam A

Section 1

1. C is correct. Though some non-felony crimes that relate to notary practice could be grounds for suspension (see *Fundamentals* (2022), at pp. 52-53), this one was not related to her practice. The serious sentence (answers B and D) is unimportant (a "felony" is about being punish*able* for a year or more, not what the actual sentence is); in any event, it would be the district court that would remove for cause (pp. 52, 638). Answer A is wrong because it suggests that only notarial failures result in suspension, when in fact a felony unrelated to notary practice leads to revocation (p. 54) and losing voter status may mean suspension (p. 52); see also our #6 below, on tactics.

2. D is correct. Legislation is the supreme law in a civil law system like Louisiana's (p. 28). Even decisions of the Louisiana supreme court (written in judicial "opinions") are not supreme law—especially if the legislature disagrees—nor binding on itself; see pp. 14, 33. (Even though they bind lower courts, p. 33, they aren't "supreme.") Attorney General Opinions are only advisory (p. 34). B is not a terrible answer, since constitutional ancillaries are treated as legislation so they are an example of the larger category that is correct. But they're just leftovers with a more controversial basis and use than simple legislation (p. 33).

> Tactic: when there is an answer that's always right (D) and another that is somewhat right (B), choose the unqualified one, the sure one. More to the point, on exams, choose the broader correct answer rather than one narrow and rare example of it: it's more broadly right, more comprehensively so. Note that "constitutional ancillaries" is the perfect distractor: it isn't right, or certainly not "best" compared to the *Fundamentals* guide-stated supremacy of legislation, but it *sounds* better, as if "constitutional" must trump mere statutes. But that's a trick because it isn't really constitutional law despite the name (p. 33).

3. A is correct. It's straight out of the list of notary functions (pp. 55, 633), and these are the well-known ones, not even the rarer ones like family meetings. But B and C are too close to the practice of law—both sound like giving legal advice (pp. 77-79). So it's not D, "all of the above."

> Tactic: if you can eliminate one option, you know it isn't "all," D. Here, B is not good even if it isn't the practice of law (but it is): the guide implies not to do this specific thing (pp. 486, 509 note 17), so they don't mean it's a legit function. The distractor is that drafting wills and family meetings are allowed functions; the problem is that giving legal advice while doing them is forbidden. C would be

> even more clearly wrong if it'd said "advise about adoption" but certainly B is wrong, so D must be, too.

4. C is correct; see p. 316. No court of any jurisdiction will enforce an absolutely null act or provision; the *type* of court is a distractor (B, D). Relative nullity (A) is about acts that violate law that protects others (p. 174), so that there could be some circumstances in which it'd be OK, e.g., that protected person consents or later confirms the act. The court may not declare a relative nullity on its own.

5. D is correct (because it is false). The supreme court (p. 27) has appellate, supervisory, *and* original jurisdiction (the latter, say, for lawyer discipline). Usually "original" means "trials," but not always. The other statements are true: A (p. 24: district courts have juries), B (pp. 15, 30), and C (p. 26).

6. B is correct, and an example of how the examiners can find answers in a non-obvious chapter. This is in ch. 30's caveats to notaries (read that chapter!), at p. 626. It's *not* expressly in ch. 7, though you can infer it from the one "conflict of interest" in that notarial-practice chapter: the bank situation noted at p. 56 which is from the statute on p. 625. That statute eliminates A as an answer. And C may sound good because community property does make couples care about "the other's" money, but it's just not enough, as pp. 625-26 makes clear, to prevent notaries from signing for a spouse without a direct interest. D is not awful as an answer since it's a legit worry (p. 626); but ultimately that passage raises the concern but says use your judgment to notarize anyway. The actual *test* to apply on the exam is whether there's a direct personal interest.

> Tactic: be literal on the exam as much as possible; don't be distracted by answers that "feel" more ethical, like D here—or your possible outrage at our #1 above that makes a person who served time still keep her commission. Examiners distract you with answers that seem like common sense (criminals can't be notaries), when you should apply the literal rule: it's about "felonies." (Hat-tip: Shane Milazzo advised me once that these examiners are literal and we should normally read their questions and options that way.) Similarly, don't overthink their question by reading something into it. I think #1 and #6 are examples of literalism.

7. B is correct. It's a classic example of appearance for a business entity, pp. 356-57. This notary-practice question is about components of a juridical act (ch. 19), and contrasts with D in that, sure, that clause is *for* or *by* a "business entity," but it's not an example of one. It's a clause we *use* for one. Literally. BTW, examiners can certainly draw questions on "notary practice" from chapters other than ch. 7, as we do here—and in #6 and #8.

8. E is correct, and a bit harder than #7 in that the answer is not so clearly stated in the study guide (see p. 345, and some answers to the guide's sample exam at back). But nothing in the fact pattern suggests Charles is signing for himself ("individually," in A—so the "all" in D is out). B and C are alternative, acceptable wordings for the same thing, so E is best.

9. D is correct. B and D say the same basic thing, but unlike for Unincorporated Associations' authorizations, the Corporate Resolution is not an authentic act (AA). See pp. 392-94 (and note that the info on such resolutions is inexplicably in the chapter on conveyances, not the one on business entities). Public info (A) is no substitute for a resolution which lists the actor's specific authority. C *would* be correct—you certainly *can* do this by pointing to a recorded resolution rather than attaching one, p. 393—but that way wasn't done in our scenario: note "original clause is used"—and that clause says it's "attached." So E isn't right, or at least best, especially saying "example given." (We doubt the examiners would clarify "example given" as much as our choice did, but still you should accept the clause given, not read into it an alternative method that *could've* been used but wasn't actually given in the clause.)

> Tactic: when you face a choice like C that's true in the abstract but doesn't fit with the facts given, look for another, "best," answer. Usually there's one that's consistent with the set-up. Also, if there's an "either A or B" type option but one of those choices is very weak while the other is strong (absolutely right), then probably they want you to choose the strong one as "best," not the "either."

10. B is correct (as "cannot"). Incorporeal immovables are not susceptible to a mortgage, the guide states (p. 279), and excludes them from its "susceptible" list (p. 291; but cross-reference there to p. 279 where it's said overtly). That list makes clear A and C *are* mortgage-able. B is surely right, so "best"; don't be tempted by the tricky possibility that trustees can't mortgage trust property. Nothing in ch. 25 says that trustees *can't*, anyway, but choose one the book for sure says.

Note: it's true that this is about mortgages, not notary practice. But be ready for a random question out of whack with the section heading—especially when they use a scenario about X (and ask mostly about X) as an excuse to ask a miscellaneous question about Y answered in a different chapter. This one's in ch. 18.

Section 2

Your library file documents will be in a separate handout they'll give you with the exam, so a little easier to flip through than how we present it here. But it's typical that there will be 1 to 3 library docs on an exam of some 75 questions.

11. C is correct, meaning it's the clearly false one. The Affidavit of Distinction is a special instrument used to *deny* identity in a specific *debt* situation (p. 578 in ch. 29, not in the affidavit section of ch. 19). It doesn't get close to doing what Miley wants here. Affidavit of One and the Same is talked about in ch. 23 about car titles (p. 437), not name changes, but it seems like an OK way to title this too (especially since that phrase is in the Body of Act). B is not perfect, since you probably would just do this in an affidavit without witnesses, but you *could* do this also in authentic form (note the witness lines), and it wouldn't seem to be an awful name for the act if you do. It's the least-best answer if it weren't so clear in the guide that Affidavit of Distinction is poor: use the answer that is clearly bad in the book, rather than the one that you have (legit) doubts about. D is OK too, since in Louisiana some things in affidavit form are called Declaration without anyone saying that's a problem—unlike in common law jurisdictions which make affidavits something done with a notary while declarations are done without. Anyway, even if D is not perfect, it's still better than C, which labels it as doing the opposite of what Miley wants to happen here: she's not distinguishing herself from anyone else. (In reality none of these captions would likely lead to the act's being invalidated, as content controls, p. 333. But the question is a search for the least worst, descriptively-fitting, label for the act as shown: that's "distinction.")

> Tactic: note the "except" at the end of the question. Or, they may ask "which one is false?" It's too easy to choose the first one you see is good and forget you're looking for the *bad* one. Circle "except" or "false" in the question while you take the exam. Read all the choices. More, we advise you to write T or F next to each choice as you go, so you don't make this mistake of forgetting the call of the question. Then choose the false one asked for. They'll ask just enough questions in the "is it false" or "except" format that you need a habit that doesn't lose an easy point on a question you actually know, by misreading it.
>
> Also, you'd never find "one and the same" in ch. 23 or "distinction" in ch. 29 the day of the exam without indexing them beforehand. The *Sidepiece* book's ch. 12 offers a complete index of the 2022 study guide, which can be written directly into the Glossary section of *Fundamentals*, to lead you the day of the exam.

12. C is correct (as false). A is true (so it's wrong, since it asks for false), as similar examples about names in the guide aren't authentic acts (AA); but mainly, name-change is *not* listed on pp. 323-25—the magic list of things that must be AA. Have that list handy exam day (and add a few entries they left out, listed in *Sidepiece* ch. 9). B is easily true (p. 358), and in fact Affiant is more specific and consistent with the caption (as asked in our set-up) than even Appearer, though Appearer is also used (e.g., p. 357) and either is acceptable. C and D raise the real issue: does name-change happen when you marry? No, says p. 197. But it also adds that either spouse may call themselves by the other's last name, so D is true. (They probably wouldn't add "wholly" as we do in D to make it clearer.)

Note that the answer isn't in ch. 19 on affidavits. The rule about names after a wedding is found in ch. 12 on persons and families. Most actual examples of affidavits are elsewhere, such as ch. 29. So an exam section's heading of "Affidavits" isn't limited at all just to the scattered pieces in ch. 19 on affidavits.

13. D is correct, since both clauses C and D are truly misstated or incomplete. This one *is* in ch. 19 (pp. 331, 358-59). Given that it's an affidavit (as the call of the question insists), it needs an evidence of oath (clause C lacks "duly sworn") and a jurat (which clause D is entirely missing). Few affidavits allow wholesale substitutes for these vital phrases. Answer A gets counted off—it's not "incomplete or misstated"—because clause B is good enough for an affidavit, which do have appearances (p. 336), but they're briefer than those for complex acts. For this "stated purpose," no property is conveyed or other severe actions where knowing a person's address or marital history matters. Most examples of affidavit in the guide have short appearances (e.g., pp. 357, 437, 539). It's the one clause that's at least satisfactory, making it the "wrong" answer.

> Tactic: beware the question that uses letters for answer-choices A to D, *and* (different) letters are part of the actual answers. It's easy to mix it up (if you think clause C is the right answer, you may pencil in the C circle; you were supposed to say *B* if so, in our example [though D is best here]). Also, note the gratuitous info that shouldn't distract you: the point about filling in a city is there to be sure that clause E wouldn't be incomplete for *that* reason if it were a choice. Why would a question clarify a clause that isn't given as a choice? Maybe because an older exam used the set-up but had different answer choices. Or just to see if your reading skills can discard extra info that doesn't matter here. But hopefully they write tight questions without a lot of unnecessary clarifications like this one.

14. A is correct, as stated on p. 331. Answer D *should* be right, and in practice just do this, but the guide discusses this exact scenario. ("Testimony" and "deposition" can be facts in an affidavit, not just court talk.) C isn't right regardless because that's not what the "de facto" doctrine does (p. 70); and it's doubtful this scenario would arise to "public injury," in B (p. 50). The guide stresses in many places the civil law is literal and enforces formalities (e.g., pp. 320, 610-12), but the "affirming signature" case is one counter-example, as is the de facto doctrine.

The examiners may not clarify so much "assume for this question only" as we do. But likely each question *means* that whether it says it or not, and tries to be independent of others. The question probably would have just started at "Miley."

> Tactic: occasionally the answer is just counterintuitive and found in the guide, not your sense of ethics. The only hint here that it's not what you'd think (or really do) is that choices B to D are a bit of the same "no" answer, though C is flat wrong as stated above. Note that some answers say "yes" but are like another "no" because of the qualification after "yes" ("but only if").

15. B is correct (as false). The nature of this affidavit is to establish her identity under both names, so it's appropriate that she would sign it twice. And she is the "one person" who signs both lines. This is even easier to see than examples in the guide of people signing as an individual and in a representative capacity (tested in their practice exam at p. 707), since she's the same person individually. A and D are incorrect (as true) because, regardless of the affidavit's home parish of Lafayette, the set-up says its venue clause is correct (Orleans). This means that it should not be signed in other parishes (though in practice it's easy to change the venue clause, even by hand). Venue is the place it's executed (p. 332). C is true because her domicile is where she *intends* to make her home, and can be Lafayette even if she has multiple residences (pp. 180-81, and expressly said p. 336).

16. D is correct. Any issue of conflict of interest is far less than one found OK on p. 626 (using test of "direct personal interest"), whether Liam is a signator (C) or Miley is sister-in-law (A). B is wrong though a bit tricky (using an exception to an exception). Ch. 7 emphasizes that those who were notaries before the state-wide exam (begun in 2005) are limited to their home parishes and some nearby ones, whereas *you* will have state-wide jurisdiction (p. 58). There's always been an exception for state-wide jurisdiction to give oaths and verify pleadings to be received in state courts (pp. 56, 634). But that doesn't mean Chris, whose commission is in Union Parish, may execute an affidavit outside Union. It's a juridical act that, like any other, would be a problem for a notary without jurisdiction.

17. D is correct. The correct conclusion for nearly all affidavits is the jurat (pp. 331, 589), with a few odd exceptions of affidavits that could be written more like an act (small successions could be; also, affidavit of distinction on pp. 579-80). This is such a normal affidavit, they'd be testing your rote use of the correct clause. Evidence of oath (B) should be stated at clause C, and the attestation clause in answer C is instead used for testaments.

18. C is correct. Affidavits require an oath so they cannot be done by witness acknowledgment (p. 328). A is wrong because most affidavits are not authentic acts (AA), and this one is specifically not on the list of AA at pp. 323-25. These witness lines shown are unneeded. Worse, "juridical acts must be authentic" is way too broad because there are plenty of juridical acts (as defined p. 315) that aren't AA, not just affidavits (like acknowledged acts, forms). B is wrong as nothing in the book ever dealing with witnesses suggests they can't be related to each other, even the strict testament rules about a witness not being too related *to the testator* (pp. 476-77). D is wrong since the perjury phrase is not a part of typical Louisiana affidavits (pp. 340-41, and see the list on p. 331 lacking it; perjury is implicit as built into taking the oath, p. 364). Because "perjury" is used a lot on affidavits in other states, it makes a good distractor if you go just by your memory of seeing that on some forms.

19. B is correct. This is a perfect example of the "de facto" doctrine (p. 70). True, his commission is invalid because of the reporting rule, but if he's in good faith, unlike the guide's example, the affidavit will be OK. It won't be fixed by having witnesses instead (D) because affidavits require an administered oath (p. 328); and anyway witnesses don't equal notary for acts that must be notarized. Usually the civil law is strict (A), as noted in #14 above, but "de facto" is a forgiving rule. C is wrong (in addition to the reason A is wrong), because the policy behind annual reports is not trivially about the public knowing your parish (anyway they can get that from the website even if you're suspended).

20. C is correct (as false). The others are routine eligibility requirements (pp. 64-66, 69, 72), and voter registration usually is, too. However, there's an exception for resident aliens, newly emphasized in recent editions of *Fundamentals* (p. 65; such new points are testable). Note that scenarios ostensibly about some act or affidavit can easily be a question about notarial practice, which is why ch. 7 is so important.

Also, don't read into the facts to strain to make option D correct, especially when C is undoubtedly correct. I say this because nothing in the question says that Chris is a non-attorney notary. If he's also an attorney, he doesn't have to post a bond (p. 65). But nothing in it says he *is* an attorney either, so don't add that to create a problem with D. Generally, between a certain answer and one conditioned on an ambiguous fact, choose the unconditional answer. (But this is not really that ambiguous: an exam about becoming a non-attorney notary likely assumes you'll read that as the default fact.)

On the other hand, if the question or answer is framed in terms of what "all notaries" must do, then they really are testing that you know that *some* of them don't—for example, the attorney-notaries don't have to post bond.

> Tactic: if the answer seems too easy because it's just a rule you learned early on or is repeated a lot in the book (such as notaries must be registered to vote), they may be testing a narrow exception. More generally, it's pretty common that they are testing *exceptions* to settled rules rather than the rule itself, because that separates the surface studier from the deep reader (or indexer). So when a basic rule comes up on exam day (even one you "know"), quickly confirm the rule in the guide yet glance around that place in the book for a possible exception.

21. A is correct (as false) because fruits of separate property are community (p. 200). B is true because he can do that (p. 205); C is true as the statement of the rule opposite of A; and D is true because that's one way to keep it separate: by a declaration of reservation, notice, and filing (pp. 200-01).

Note that it's pretty common for scenarios about some act to then raise an unrelated question or two about community versus separate property (you already know the people involved so they can veer off). Also note that the set-up doesn't give away it's "separate property" and you have to figure that out first, by "legal regime" and "in 2016," checking their (actual) marriage date in the library document.

22. A is correct, as a standard benefit of being usufructary: "civil" fruits like rents (pp. 92, 103-04). The other answers give someone else an interest. Miley is just the naked owner (on a wrecking ball), or she and Liam would be if somehow it was community.

Note: don't get the rules about separate-property fruits (#21) mixed up with the ones about usufructs. They could test them in the same scenario to see if you can keep them straight.

23. D is correct. They're all incidentals that the usufructary is responsible to pay (p. 109). This is one is pretty easy if you can find the guide page on point.

> Tactic: if "all of the above" is an option, you only have to be sure two are true—or *not* be 100% certain one of the choices is false. Again write T or F at each answer, as you do for a "which is false?"-type question, to be sure you're answering the whole thing and not just picking the first option that looks right ("I remember the example of property taxes so I'll fill in B.").

24. E is correct. D is wrong because this isn't about Liam's usufruct (even if it were community, but even then choice D cannot assume she died intestate), nor does this involve, as in C, a right of habitation (that's not a usufruct, but also isn't inheritable, anyway, if the question were about the usufructary's death). A is wrong because no time limits were stated in the original act (#22), but anyway there's no default rule of ten years for a time limit. B is the distractor because it's easy to mix this statement up with the clear rule that the usufruct terminates on the death of the usufructary (p. 105), but here Miley, the deceased, is the naked owner. Nothing in ch. 9 suggests the usufruct ends with the owner's death, and in fact property is routinely transferred or donated subject to the usufruct (p. 101).

Section 3

25. C is correct. No rule anywhere in the guide governs limitations about what parish appearers sign in. Limits are on certain notaries (without state-wide jurisdiction, but Katrina has that) and where acts are *filed*. Signators often travel to a notary not in their parish. They don't have to own property there (A) to affect it by acts signed elsewhere. Succession is not based on where the will was signed (D). C is a straightforward statement that is true so it's best even over B, which could be true if it's misread—but note it makes the state-wide notary somehow control a rule about where appearers must sign. That could be a sloppy way of saying the state-wide notary jurisdiction allows Katrina to sign anywhere, therefore it lets signators sign there too—but really the jurisdiction rule is not about the issue raised in the call of the question, which worries about *Cal's* home and Cal signing it, not Katrina Katz. But even if you read choice B as a clever way at getting at *her* signing, it's not as clear a reading as C applies.

> Tactic: if two answers seem right, but one is a straightforward, true statement, while one makes you infer something in the option's wording, choose the direct one. Also note that a section on wills sometimes includes a few questions about notary practice (ch. 7), juridical acts (ch. 19), or community property (ch. 12).

26. D is correct. They are examples of legatees that can be excluded. Jan is over 24 so that's the same as Nan being 26 (p. 479). Neither is disabled (pp. 479-80), so any option having a forced heir is wrong. C is a distractor that gets into the nomenclature of forced "heirs," though that rule actually only applies to testate situations (involving "legatees," not "heirs"—they often test the difference). But whatever oddity is presented in "forced heir" (and it's not so odd if you remember that they're just saying a will can't get rid of some donations that would happen if you die intestate—to heirs), it has nothing to do with whether Jan and Nan are forced heirs. It's a true statement that makes no difference here.

> Tactic: if one of the options seems to be a true statement in the abstract but doesn't answer the concern presented in the call of the question—here, terminology trivia doesn't answer whether they can be left out—it's probably wrong or not the best answer.

27. B is correct. This is the place for the attestation clause for the witnesses (p. 509), not the conclusion (in A and D). And if it's signed in Orleans Parish, the place should not be Baton Rouge, in C (even if that's his home). Note the examiners often test correct wording of clauses (such as ch. 19 details), and in fact the August 2020 and January 2022 exams had a whole section on juridical acts, their appearance clauses, and other phrasings. *This* clause is found in ch. 24.

> Tactic: write out a few very common acts into your *Fundamentals*. The writing-out process makes you look for the proper clauses. The testament example need not be written out because the authors provide a great model at the end of ch. 24 (pp. 507-09). Looking at that would make answering this question easy.

28. *A is correct*, applying the rule at p. 502. B and C alter the document after it's executed and could cause a problem (like the strict order of signing issue (pp. 610-11); certainly the notary can't write more on the will! D is incorrect in that the first page, whether from an early draft, is what was read and signed so it may not be ideal but it's valid. D is tempting because we do read the wills process strictly in many ways other than this date flexibility. Anyway, this minor date discrepancy, easily proved in the succession, won't invalidate the will (so the examiners may make it harder by giving a larger date span, but look for whether the true date can be readily ascertained).

29. *D is correct*, as stated in a case (jurisprudence) on p. 503. Even initials don't substitute for a signature, p. 500, so C is wrong. A and B make sense given one reason to require signature-at-bottom, and other rules in ch. 24, but they simply aren't the rule that case held. Knowing the policy behind the rule would make you overthink the answer, choosing A. The key is *finding* this rule in the study guide. For some reason it's not in the "Signature of testator" section of the book, rather a few pages later. Write a note on p. 500 to "see p. 503 if 2-sided paper."

> Tactic: unfortunately, it's pretty common for the examiners to test a rule that is stated in the guide at an odd place, not under its natural heading. There's a premium on adding cross-references into the guide, as spelled out for you in *Sidepiece* ch. 13, or make note of several such instances as you read the guide.

Section 4

30. *C is correct.* It's not a pet trust, pp. 526-28, nor a counterletter, pp. 394-95, though it may *seem* like either of those would fit (especially "counterletter" if you don't know its actual meaning). *This* is a contract, of sorts. In this case it creates strictly personal obligations (p. 155), since it requires each to provide a service to the other that can't easily be paid off by others: it's expecting each one to do it themselves. "Exchange," option B, doesn't mean the ordinary use of the word, which would seem to fit, but is a special form of conveyance of property discussed in ch. 21 (pp. 377-79).

Note that this section heading would likely be "Contracts" or similar, but we did not want to give away too much in the title. Anyway, most of it doesn't test the contracts chapter, 11. And it's common for the examiners to have the answer-options to come from disparate parts of the book even if the question fits under the main test grouping ("agreement," so predictably ch. 11), here using counter-letter (ch. 21), exchange (ch. 21), and pet trust (ch. 25).

> Tactic: it's easy to test whether you read the guide by asking about legal terms that have a different meaning from their common understanding. For example,

"vulgar substitutions" aren't bad (p. 481); "real right" is not really about real estate (p. 271); "confusion" is a term of art for predial servitudes (p. 126); and "procès verbal" is a written report (p. 531). A smart but unprepared test-taker would get it wrong by using common parlance. You already know that naked owners may not be nudists. No, this pet agreement is not an "exchange," even though of course they are exchanging chores. So, while you re-read the study guide, make a mental note any time a legal term jumps out at you as being counterintuitive from what you'd *think* the term means. Maybe make a list of funny "misused" legal words to look over the day before the exam and have somewhere accessible in the guide itself. Otherwise, usufruct.

31. E is correct. Private acts (A) do not self-authenticate (they must be proved in court, p. 325), but acknowledged and authentic acts do, pp. 319, 327. A question about obligations, or *any* scenario, can come back to the basics of juridical acts in ch. 19. See also p. 160 ("proof of obligtions").

32. B is correct (as wrong). The others are acceptable ways to make it be self-proving. A is signing it again but this time making it in authentic form; C is one way to do a private act duly acknowledged; and D is the other way. See pp. 327-28. B is not either version of an acknowledged act, plus without two witnesses at each signing (not mentioned in the option), it's not authentic either. The only reason this question may be hard is that the two forms of acknowledgment are confusing. C and D state them correctly.

33. A is correct. This is what a counterletter does (pp. 394-95), though it's disfavored. The trade-off may create personal obligations, but the extra document is not that. It's a modification of the contract. And it may be forbidden, but that's not the term to define it—plus it's not a "substitution" as the law uses that term, p. 481, even if it sounds like they substituted words (like how secret codes are often made via "substitution").

Again, learn the legal terms of art and beware being tricked by your common use of a phrase. BTW, vulgar substitutions are OK (#30), so the phrase "forbidden vulgar substitution" is itself a red flag that D may be wrong.

34. D is correct. The counterletter or agreement won't be enforced if it's against law or public morality (pp. 173-74, 316), *absolutely*. It's not just to protect someone who could consent to the burden, as in a relative nullity (B), p. 174. A is wrong: it's true that it's disfavored (p. 395) and a court *may* refuse to enforce it for that, but our question is emphatic that it's unenforceable. C is wrong because notarizing a counterletter doesn't get at its essential problem; and notarizing this null act doesn't make it any more valid.

Tactic: if one answer is certainly or always right (emphatically right, or by definition), but one is sometimes or conditionally so, choose the certain one (see #25 above). That seems an obvious tip, but under pressure here, A may sound right because it *is* a true statement—it just isn't the reason a court would give ("hey you used the wrong format when you made your illegal arms babysitting deal").

Section 5

35. B is correct. It's remunerative to compensate for past services, pp. 149-51. Despite some lingo seeming to place a future burden on donee ("keeps working"), this isn't onerous in the classic sense of a gift with *future* strings attached, p. 150 (distinguishing the two). This is really about the past up to the present. This might be a *dation* if there were a sum certain owed for those past services (pp. 151, 379); the question's "roughly" part is there to make sure it's not a fixed sum certain—and also that it's not a donation in disguise, p. 151 (worth at least 2/3 of the value of the past work—a sub-rule they do test on; here, the natural inference from "roughly" is that it's equivalent in value within that 2/3 margin). Any of these alternatives would not require authentic form (pp. 148, 151), so choice A is wrong. As a remunerative donation, then, the two witnesses are not required, p. 148, as is normally required for a gratuitous one.

> Tactic: they often test the difference in these forms of land conveyance—and the question may well come down to whether they use the present or past tense. Take the tense literally so as not to fight the distinction they're drawing between onerous and remunerative donations, in particular.

36. D is correct. When is a donation effective? When donee accepts, not just when the act is signed (p. 134), so A is wrong. Usually that means written acceptance (C), as on p. 135. But there's a subtle way to accept immovables without a writing saying so, which includes encumbering the property in a recorded act (B), noted on pp. 135-36 (the parish is where the property is situated). But *not* just by moving in and possessing it (for immovables), as previously allowed. A related question: can a donation be signed by donor without donee there? Of course; donee can accept later in writing, for example, as in C. It doesn't invalidate the original act; and the acceptance need not be an authentic act (p. 146), as was once the rule—even if the donation itself must be AA.

> Tactic: they do test subtle exceptions. So during the exam, find the place in the book with the clear rule you remember (donations need written acceptance) then look nearby for a weird exception. This one makes sense: the filing of the mortgage is even more dominating than writing "I accept," and it gives public notice in the mortgage records of who now owns it, easily found by searching title.

37. A is correct. The government owns "private things" when it's acting like private actors do, buying cars and office buildings so they can do their work (p. 83). It's not "common" (B) because that's things not owned by anyone, such as air (p. 82); it's not "public" (D), counterintuitively, because that means property owned by the government for the open and free use of everyone, like rivers and streets (pp. 82-83). Civil fruits (C) are not about this situation at all; they mean revenues derived from a thing by law, such as rents or dividends (p. 92).

> Tactic: even on what looks like an obvious answer, it's best to look quickly into the study guide during the exam to confirm your answer. This one's counterintuitive from your ordinary understanding of "public" and so may be an easy point missed if you don't check and find out it's actually "private."

74

12

Answers and Explanations: Exam B

Section 1

1. C is correct (as the false answer asked for in the call of the question). A is true because Nana is not a legatee or in any conflict of interest and can be a witness. See *Fundamentals* (2022), pp. 348, 476-77, 499. B is true since he generally doesn't have to leave any of *his* estate to his wife, though she still owns her own interest in the house (so it's not part of his estate), pp. 450, 484. D is true because Dora is not supposed to be a witness, as a legatee too, but the effect of that is not to invalidate the will but to limit her to the amount she'd get as an heir if he had no will, pp. 348, 476. That's the same as what he left her (p. 445). So, C is false in that the will remains valid. The part about the appointment of executor is a bit of a distractor because while true, it's not at issue here but nonetheless doesn't change the essential fact that the will is valid.

2. D is correct. See p. 477, making clear that appointing an executor is not naming a legacy as such. So, a notary even if considered a witness of sorts is not ineligible to serve as executor (it's fairly common). A and C are wrong in that they say the will is invalid; even if it was leaving a legacy to the notary, it would not invalidate the will (just their legacy), pp. 348-49, 476. B is doubly wrong in that a notary *or a witness* can be an executor, p. 477.

3. C is correct (for being false). That statement is a correct capacity for a test-tube fetus if there was *no will*, pp. 447-48, just like D accurately says. A is true as the basic rule for fetuses under a will, p. 475. B is true because any legatee who is a forced heir will receive one quarter of the estate if there is a total of two forced heirs (they split half of the estate), p. 479. Note that at age 19, Dora is forced too.

4. B is correct, as it's a classic example of a particular legacy (pp. 471 and 508 note 12). It's not the other kinds of legacies in A and D. C is potentially not a terrible answer in that he *could* be giving in trust to the museum (as in pp. 528-29), but we'd need more language about the ownership relationship and beneficiary and all that to know that's what was intended. Just because it is a donation to a nonprofit doesn't make it a charitable *trust*. It's a bit of a distractor because the museum may be a charity, but tactically if there's an answer (B) that's true by definition, don't read new facts into the gift and strain to make C work. Generally, don't add facts anyway, to turn an iffy answer into your "right" one.

5. D is correct. Mere wishes or preferences don't clearly *give*, pp. 501-02. Precatory words are not enough (unless everyone wants to honor them). C is wrong as the opposite of that, treating it as if it were clearly gifted. Better words to make that happen are "give," "donate at my death," "bequeath," etc. Option A *sounds* right because usually legacies can't be made by incorporating external documents (like a list of specific bequests), pp. 503-04, but the exception to that is mere identifying documents, like the extra contact info here. B is flatly wrong because that is not how a will registry works, pp. 505-06.

> Tactic: this example illustrates how one question can raise several different issues by the answer-options given. Not all the answers here are about precatory words that don't clearly "give." Different pages in ch. 24 come up. Be ready to move around within the study guide even for one question, and don't assume the different answers fall on nearby pages (though in this case they happen to).

6. A is correct. It's fine to gift something conditioned on someone being able and willing to take it, then also name a back-up recipient if that condition fails (pp. 481, 486). Naming a back-up is considered a vulgar substitution, meaning it's permitted (despite how "vulgar" may mislead you). A *forbidden* substitution (B) would be like giving it to Nana on condition that when she dies, it goes to Tess (pp. 140, 481). No, because if it's left to Nana, she owns it. She can do what she wants with it. She may hate Tess for all I know. Andy can't control that re-gifting from the grave. C is wrong because this substitution is OK but not all of them are (above). D is wrong because, though it states the problem of forbidden substitutions (as in B), that problem doesn't exist for vulgar ones (this one). BTW, D is a little off in using the lingo of "naked" which is more about usufructs.

> Tactic: beware the answer, like D, which is a true statement in the abstract (it's true by itself), but doesn't really apply to the facts or problem in the question set-up. (D is not incorrect, except there's no problem in *this* case that a testator is controlling the re-gifting from the grave. He just made a back-up plan if the one who *could've* owned it turns it down.) When that happens, usually there's a better answer—one more applicable to the facts—available to choose. Pick it.

7. B is correct. This is a stated example of a legal mortgage (one arising by law), p. 287, though the answer is oddly found in the chapter on mortgages, not in the wills chapter, 24. Writing a cross-reference or index entry into the guide could help, but otherwise on the day of the exam you could look up "mortgage" and "pledge" to, hopefully, see this answer is in the book (and it's not pledge or a conventional mortgage—the latter reserved for mortgage by agreement, by and large, not arising by law). D *sounds* best, since it is something that gets done in a judicial proceeding (like a judge requires it), but it's not right. This question would be much harder if choice D said "suretyship" because that answer seems to be better than "legal mortgage"—if you didn't find this answer at p. 287. You'd really need to find "legal mortgage" in the guide to eliminate it on exam day . . . and in the process you'd actually see it's correct according to the book.

8. C is correct. The distractor, A, *seems* correct in that she's still a forced heir because the lack of communication is too short after turning 18 (p. 490). But Andy died intestate (the effect of an invalid will), so forced heirship one way or the other is irrelevant, p. 480. B is wrong for the same error, applying forced-heir law to an intestate situation. (The same question could be asked under a *valid* will where he disinherits her, then A would be good [though the actual time of "only lasted a year" may be off, if she's been 19 a while].) D is wrong in that "unworthy successors" (p. 457) aren't the same as "kids you can disinherit," plus lack of communication for a year or two isn't close to making the kid "unworthy."

> Tactic: it's easy to mix up terms and rules for intestate successions with those for testate ones. They may well test you on that. Knowing ch. 24 cold helps, but particularly being able to confirm answers test-day in the right part of the chapter matters (first part is intestate, rest of chapter is testate). Here, you'd quickly notice that the section on disinherison is far after the intestate one.

9. *A is correct.* That's exactly how intestate succession works when there is a surviving child or grandchild, p. 448, with the spouse receiving a usufruct on the half of the house she doesn't already own, p. 451. B is wrong since the whole house is not Andy's to give, just his half. C is wrong because, in intestate successions, the spouse Tess will not inherit if there are favored heirs like Dora, p. 451 (though Tess of course keeps her half of the house—that's not "inheriting" it). D is wrong because intestate successions certainly have usufructs for surviving spouses (if anything, it's more easily modified by will, pp. 483-84).

10. *B is correct.* The examiners often ask you to value an estate at the time of death and sort out former community property from separate property. It can be asked in intestate or testate situations, or by eligibility for a small succession. In this example, his estate is half the house + vase + stock. See pp. 204, 450-52. The set-up made clear there's no fruits of the stock which may be community. The question could be harder if some of the individual items were more questionable as separate property than the vase and stock are here. The big distractor is italicizing *gross*, which may make you think we mean to include the full value of the house (so, choose C). But "gross" has a particular meaning for this issue, p. 542, just meaning before you deduct debts. Don't let the italics steer you wrong.

11. *C is correct.* This situation begs for using the succession by affidavit (ch. 27). They sometimes ask you to think of a solution to a problem rather than labeling it for you. This question makes you do that. It also tests your ability to locate that process in the right statute (they may have one question that's a vestige of the time when a part of the exam was locating civil code articles). Counterintuitively, small successions are in the Code of Civil Procedure (see p. 542) rather than books of the Civil Code, p. 30. B is especially wrong because other successions law is not in "Persons" but in the book about acquiring things. A is wrong because small successions are fine with community property and in fact require the affidavit to specify the community interest and the spouse's usufruct, p. 544. D is wrong because, although the value is under the gross-value cap, non-attorney notaries may not prepare succession papers; that's the unauthorized practice of law, p. 546. (On the actual exam, if small successions come up, they tend to have one question that makes you calculate whether the estate is eligible for this procedure by making you do the math from our previous question, then comparing that to the current cap—now, $125,000. It's been only a few years since Louisiana law raised the cap, so the 125k number is one they expect you to know.)

> Tactic: we recognize that nothing in the set-up said the notary wasn't an attorney, such that D could be OK if the estate value fits. But you shouldn't read into a mention of a notary that they're a lawyer too, unless the question clearly says so. It's another example of over-reading the question, as by answering in your head, "Choice D would be right *if* he's a lawyer, so I'll pick it." You added facts that are not natural inferences suggested from the facts. You rewrote the question.

12. B is correct (as false). Succession by affidavit (called "small succession" here so as to not give away too easily it's an affidavit) need not be an authentic act (though that's another format one can use). It can be in *affidavit* form (with more than one signer, unusual for an affidavit), thus two witnesses are not required to the signing, so B is false (note that this act is rightly missing on the list of AA at pp. 323-25). But in the unusual situation here where Dora is the only relative, so doesn't have a second heir or spouse to sign too, there's an exception that she needs to bring one *fact* witness (not just a signing witness) to verify the facts of the affidavit. It could be a neighbor or Dora's spouse. See p. 544 (para. B). So, C is true. A and D are true items to list on the act or affidavit, right off the long list of required details at pp. 543-44.

> Tactic: remember when the question calls for a "false" option, writing T or F next to each option keeps you from mixing it up and giving a true, wrong answer.

13. D is correct. One who creates and funds a trust is the "settlor," p. 510. The other roles are in ch. 25, too, except "naked owner" is about usufructs, not trusts. This question may seem too easy, but expect one question as direct as the trust roles here; or with the roles in usufructs; or with "heir" (intestate) vs. "legatee" (testate). But don't expect two such low-hanging fruit, as we do here (#14). They also may test whether you know that "mortgagor" is not bank but the borrower. You'd be wise to create a short list accessible in the book on exam day defining commonly used words that are easy to mix up, such as: heir/legatee; principal/mandatary; lessor/lessee; mortgagor/mortgagee; and drawer/drawee/payee.

Note the confusing fact that in the context of trusts, the "principal" is not a person (as it is for mandates and other relationships) but is the trust funds, the *res*. That term would be easy to test on, but mix up, thinking the settlor is the "principal" when instead *property* is.

> Tactic: the examiners are unlikely to be as clear as we are here (twice) that the will is otherwise valid. They're more likely to just start talking about the added clause creating a trust. Apparently you should assume the will is otherwise valid when answering questions about the trust now added to it (even if some previous question was about it being invalid or there are reasons in the original scenario

or library doc it may not be valid), unless there is something in *this* question that calls into question the will, too. Sometimes it would seem that the honest answer should be "whatever trust provision you're adding now won't work because it's part of a will that I established three questions ago is invalid as written." But they won't give that as an option and they appear to mean "assume it's valid."

14. *C is correct*, since Sue is trustee, while Dora is beneficiary (apparently both a principal and income one, if you could rent the *res* on WatchBnB). See p. 511.

15. *C is correct.* Nothing in the chapter on trusts suggests trustee and settlor must be different people (it's a common way of setting up a trust), and they even make clear that the settlor may be beneficiary (p. 518). A and B are wrong by confusing the controversial rule about whether a donor can reserve a usufruct to himself (pp. 132-33). D is wrong because, while the trustee *is* the true owner (which makes Louisiana trust law so different, p. 510), it's OK if that's the person who settled the trust in the first place: he dispossessed it to himself, changing roles for himself (just like someone in an individual capacity could donate land to himself as owner of an LLC).

Tactic: when two answers are diametrical opposites (like A and B here are, somewhat), it's tempting to assume the correct choices have reduced to those two. Often that's strategically so. But that only works if the two opposites relate to the actual topic being asked. They could be off on their own tangent, like here dealing with complex donor/donee roles and usufruct. Neither is responsive to this question, which is about trust roles. They're both distractors, even if they contain some statements that are true on their own.

16. *E is correct.* Those are the ways in which a trust is created, pp. 511-12 (plus the acknowledgment could be made by settlor instead of one of the witnesses). It doesn't *require* an authentic act, so B is wrong. Even if you can't find the ch. 25 page that discusses these methods (which is, oddly, under "forms of trusts" not "creation of trusts"), notice that creating a trust isn't on the pp. 323-25 magic list of AA-only acts, plus it *is* on the acknowledgment list, p. 327.

Note that C alone—a true statement for inter vivos trusts—is something of a distractor in that, if your mind is stuck on the facts from the previous question (where it's clearly inter vivos), you may eliminate a testamentary method (A) as valid, too. This question simply says that Andy wants to establish a trust. Even A (treating it as only in a will just because the original scenario was a will) doesn't preclude alternatively setting it up as a trust inter vivos. So the best answer that reads the set-up of this question in the most natural way (he just wants to set up a trust, tell him how) is E.

17. *B is correct.* All of the actual, active roles can be played by juridical persons like corporations (e.g., pp. 513, 518), as commonly happens when a "First Bank & Trust" serves as trustee for a named beneficiary. But the trust itself is not a juridical person (p. 510), so A is wrong. D may sound like it's about the rule that trusts are not juridical persons, but it's about the trust*ee* who actually owns the *res* (principal). Remember that the trust doesn't own it.

18. A is correct. "A refusal of an interest in an inter vivos trust must be evidenced by an authentic act" (p. 525). It may be true in practice that one could simply 'not take possession' to kill the deal (C), but the question asked about *proof* of that refusal, which requires AA. That makes sense: whoever is going to get the watch next needs to do more than just show that the first recipient wound up not having it. (Notice that such refusal is listed on p. 324 in that list of AA-only acts.) Because a simple writing won't suffice (that's for refusing *testamentary* trusts, also p. 525), therefore B and D are wrong.

Note that, again, the actual exam may not be so clear as to tell you to assume the capacity/role issues of the previous question aren't a problem. They may ask this question without revisiting that issue. Unless specifically given it as an option, don't focus for this question on the possibility that the gift fails because it never was valid in the first place (for some reason having to do with capacity). Treat the questions as relatively independent except for the most basic core facts they must have in common to make sense of the current question. They probably tend to mean that each question is fairly independent and could be asked out of order.

19. B is correct. This is the ultimate effect of termination of the income beneficiary's interest, as stated on p. 520. (Though the fact pattern doesn't label it for you, Nana is an income beneficiary while Dora is principal beneficiary. The owner is Ace & Barrow and Dora is certainly *a* beneficiary, so C is wrong.) They are not successive income beneficiaries (D), as that term of art is not used just because realistically in this instance Dora "succeeds" to the income after Nana dies (p. 518), and there was no designation mentioned of whether anyone else would start getting the income after Nana dies (how successive beneficiaries are set up in the instrument). A is wrong because it's the other way around (principal could be invaded to help out an income beneficiary, pp. 520-21), and anyway that power is not automatically assumed but is just something a trust instrument *could* do (p. 520: "trust instrument may provide").

> Tactic: choose the best answer even if none is perfect. In this instance, it may be a little more complicated how "the trust terminates" after Nana dies. It could be that Dora starts getting the income while also being principal beneficiary before the trust itself terminates. But the eventual result is what's stated in B, and it's stated in the guide that a principal beneficiary generally gets no benefit until termination; so B is certainly a better answer than the other ones, which are wrong by definition. If an answer is true and consistent with a quote from the book but you can think of a complicated way it's not true, consider it true—especially if the alternatives are irrelevant to the facts or have some definitional flaw in them.

20. E is correct. If you don't like the law's default of who decides, you'll have to designate who will dispose of your remains using a notarized instruction (though not necessarily only a notarized *testament*), pp. 495-96. That leaves out olographic wills, since they're not notarized (p. 495), which is an odd hole in the law, and testable (especially since the section on remains is recently expanded, such as the distinction between "how" remains are handled vs. "who" decides).

> Tactic: note that the question never says "disposition of remains," which is the guide's heading. So, be careful when you index, or use the index or table of contents during the exam, to think of alternative ways to say the same thing. (You may want a second entry under "cremation.") Another example is community property: some of its content is under "legal regime." Or how "bond" may fall under "suretyship," or "affidavit of correction" may be under "act of correction."

The examiners may describe facts in such a way that part of what they're testing, before you apply the law (and that's tested too), is to recognize what the issue is. For example, they may say that "John conveys to Betty with no strings attached a gift of a house." They don't have to use the phrase "gratuitous donation" to then in effect test you on knowing that's what they just described—before then testing you on the rules about such a donation, such as this kind requires an AA.

Section 2

21. B is correct. It is a bilateral document establishing the agency relationship, so it's a mandate rather than a (unilateral) procuration (D). See p. 250. There aren't a lot of indicia of an actual two-way contract, but the fact that the document includes the agents' acceptance signed with it makes it more likely that it's a mandate. There are no specific provisions authorizing health care decisions (and there'd have to be, p. 252), so it's not A. C would make sense if it were appointing an attorney-at-law rather than an attorney-in-fact. That agents "represent the principal in legal relations," p. 248, is not the same as calling it a "legal representation." But in any event, it's so clearly a *mandate* that B is best.

> Tactic: almost anything that makes the non-attorney notary or a party sound like they are practicing law or giving legal advice will likely be considered by the examiners to be the "unauthorized practice of law," given how many times in the study guide you're warned not to do that. Don't bite on answers that empower people, including a notary not clearly also a lawyer, to do lawyer-like actions.

22. A is correct. She is the principal, the one who sets up the mandate and empowers the representative/agent. See p. 250. C is wrong because the recipient of the power is called the mandatary. Powers of attorney such as mandates have nothing to do with creating trusts, and the actors don't include trustees (D). B is wrong because this is not an affidavit so the appearer is not an affiant, nor can an affidavit be made for someone else by a mandatary (p. 365, in the chapter on "Oaths" instead of in ch. 15 on mandates; so, write this rule on p. 251).

23. A is correct. She has capacity even at 14 to serve as witness, if she has "proper understanding" (p. 348), which the facts apparently establish here. (The age floor is 16 for a *will*.). There's no real problem with Linda being a relative

(p. 348), at least not "automatically," so one would not say she is "prohibited from serving in this role."

24. E is correct. None of these is a real problem (even if some of them aren't a problem if left out, either). Venue clauses can be this data-rich (p. 332); in many situations an appearance clause may need a marital-change clause, but here there's no transfer of immovable property (p. 340), while this act *has* a good statement of marital *status* (p. 337); it's certainly OK for this to have witnesses (be an AA) even if no one needs that to lease a place for Samantha (they may use it for other purposes that *are* AA, so it makes sense to go ahead and have witnesses); and nothing in ch. 15 states that there cannot be co-agents (it's pretty common). D is not a bad answer because the guide could be clearer that such multiple representatives (not just successive ones, or replacements) are OK, the way co-executors can be and often are.

25. B is correct. A mandate or procuration must be in authentic form if it is authorizing an act that itself must be AA (p. 250). Here, a gratuitous donation of an immovable requires an AA (p. 146), so the power of attorney must be in that form. But there are many other actions that can be empowered without an authentic act, so A is wrong. Both C and D are wrong in making requirements that may exist for the transferring document be required in the mandate, too. While the mandate must specify expressly the power to donate (p. 252), that doesn't require that the *who* be named in advance. The donation itself will need a property description (p. 383), but this power of attorney doesn't.

> Tactic: two rules seem to be tested a lot if donation is covered at all: (1) If the mandate will be used by the agent to donate an immovable, that power must be expressly stated in this document, not just "convey" or "transfer." (2) Powers of attorney used to make authentic acts must themselves be AA, too. Look for them.

26. D is correct. Applying the rule noted just above, recent editions of the study guide have emphasized that donation must be expressly listed as a power of the mandatary (p. 252). It's stated in a slightly indirect way by noting that the type of conveyance (i.e., donation) is missing, but that's the rule in action. A is wrong because 'paragraph B' states the conclusion clause well for this type of act. B is wrong because the principal can sign outside of her parish of domicile (folks often travel to a notary); this question doesn't involve the limitations on where a notary of limited jurisdiction may sign (ch. 7). C is wrong—or at least not the best answer compared to the certain requirement in D that donation be expressly authorized—because the agency role need not be accepted in the document itself nor at the time of the original act. This must be true since a power of attorney need not have any acceptance at all at the time of signing—then it's a procuration (p. 250: "when he accepts ... is ordinarily a mandate"). So, C is not a perfect answer in that this could now be a procuration instead of a mandate (though it's probably a mandate once Lori accepts, anyway, p. 249 para. (d)); but even that form is otherwise "valid to accomplish the intended purpose" as the question asks. The fatal flaw is in D.

27. B is correct (as not proper). If she's properly registered to vote in Bossier, her domicile isn't Caddo. See p. 337 (and recall that the same is true for your home parish as a notary). Temporarily living in Bossier with intent to return to Caddo once repairs are done makes Caddo her domicile (A), as her "habitual place of residence" (p. 180). The principal's daughter's home seems irrelevant (C), and the book even contemplates (p. 180) that a child may live elsewhere. D is wrong (in that it doesn't preclude Caddo from being domicile), because her accident doesn't change her domicile, just (at most) her residence for the time being. Nothing in the facts indicates her intent to stay in Washington Parish.

This question could be cagier if it didn't say "appearer's domicile" but merely hinted that's the issue by asking whether the "appearance clause is correctly stated," making the test-taker see that the problem would be "domicile" if she voted elsewhere.

28. C is correct. Because the witnesses didn't observe the original signing by Samantha, it's not authentic. So, assuming for this question that the document gives express authority for an act, which of the acts doesn't require AA? Credit sale. At least without "confession of judgment" language in it, p. 390 (and the facts don't say it has that), a credit sale is like an act of cash sale in that it need not be AA. It *does* have to be in writing (p. 366), which it is. The other acts must be authentic (see pp. 323-25), namely designation of tutor in A (p. 588); statement of authority in B (pp. 394, 571); and concurrence to adult adoption in D (p. 575).

This is a common way for the examiners to ask you which act needs to be AA: by giving you a document not in authentic form, then asking: is it valid? Here, the question doesn't focus on the requirement of express authority, saying it had that.

29. D is correct. See pp. 251-52 for powers that are OK if expressly provided; they include the power to "enter into a compromise" (B), which is lawyer talk for "settlement." Not noted on the list, but elsewhere (p. 121) is the authority to create predial servitudes. Both A and C are such predial servitudes (pp. 115, 119).

This is a question about power of attorney that turns on servitude law. It shows how you won't be able to answer the question by sticking to ch. 15 on mandates. It'd help for this specific example that you write "create predial servitudes" in the list around p. 252 and cross-reference to p. 121.

30. D is correct. With a disclosed mandate and an undisclosed principal, as here, the agent binds herself personally for the performance of the contract. See p. 257. That would not be true if she disclosed the principal's name (p. 256), in which option A would be correct. B is wrong because the book never suggests that the store has some duty to identify the principal, but if it did, clearly that was not done here. C sounds like it could be the rule, and makes sense, but under C.C. art. 3018, it just isn't correct.

31. E is correct. Both A and B are "correct" in being prohibited uses of the power of attorney (pp. 251 [adding that you can't have two people in one will either], 365). So, E (both A and B) is "best." Also forbidden to representatives are marriage and adult adoption. With express authority to donate (and if the mandate is done as an authentic act), donating an immovable *is* proper (pp. 251-52).

> Tactic: you may want to make a list somewhere accessible on exam day (perhaps top of p. 247?) of four things you can't do via power of attorney ("POA"):
> • will • marriage • adoption • affidavit

32. C is correct. See p. 260. This is a subtle exception to the general rule that mandates terminate when either the principal or the agent dies (p. 258). A couple pages later they clarify that the agent can finish something they started, to protect the deceased's interest. Imagine if the renovation removed the roof, Samantha dies, and Jodi cannot deal with the roofers to finish the work. B then is a distractor because it does state a general rule (except for the "fully"), but C is better because it is a more precise rule. Note that without the word "fully," one could argue that both B and C are true. A is doubly wrong in that it waits to terminate the mandate until *both* die, and there's no such rule. D is a decent distractor because it sounds like it *could* be the rule and may even be a better rule. But nothing in ch. 15 or ch. 24 suggests that executor takes over from mandatary.

33. A is correct. This is about juridical acts and appearances, ch. 19. It's clear the principal is listed first, though information on both actors is needed (pp. 335, 356). Consider that it's still Samantha's mortgage, so the bank is mostly interested in *her* information, but also needs to see Jodi's authority to represent her.

34. A is correct (as not acceptable). When signing in a representative capacity, the agent/mandatary doesn't sign the principal's name. The signer is the agent, so their name is the one on the line. If you don't already infer this from the guide, consider that all the other ways here are explicitly adequate ways to sign on the line (pp. 344-45), including printed non-cursive writing (C) and using initials (D). The guide implies that even a squiggle that can't be made out to be Hatch would work in most cases as long as the identity can be ascertained (p. 345). Even "Jodi" would do. The distractor here is that you may confuse the strict rule on full names (what goes below the signature line) with the lax standards for a signature. Compare pp. 336, 637: "S.S. Smith" is not a full name, by statute.

35. B is correct. The default in our state is that powers of attorney are "durable," whether they say so or not (C). They don't terminate just because the principal is now incapacitated (p. 258); Jodi can keep working on Samantha's behalf (Lori, too, since we're back to the original act). A and D are distractors because they are methods, not to keep a mandate going as the question is about, but to declare someone's incapacity in order to activate a conditional procuration (p. 249). So, the question is about when the mandate ends (by Samantha's death but not her incapacity; by Jodi's death *or* interdiction), not about when the power begins if the original act only made it happen once the principal becomes disabled. (FWIW, D is worse than A, in that such a trigger to conditional procuration must be AA.)

36. D is correct. Louisiana corporation names must have at least English letters (p. 561). Don't be distracted (A) by the oft-tested rule that *articles of incorporation* must be in English (p. 559). There's no problem that the name says "Co." instead of other common suffixes (p. 561), so C is wrong. B is wrong because the guide's mention of a trade name registered with SOS (p. 561), easily misunderstood if you read too fast, is about not allowing a name that overlaps with a trade name so registered, like someone else's corporate name they claimed first.

13

Answers and Explanations: Exam C

Section 1

1. A is correct. See *Fundamentals* (2022), pp. 60, 152. The distractors about *when* to record (B and C) kick in if the notary is the one to record it (pp. 59-60). D seems like it should be the right answer, that there's some continuing obligation on the notary to take reasonable steps to assume the recording system that the instrument got into it. But there's not one if the express terms on the instrument provide for the notary to deliver the instrument to a signator or even a third party. BTW, this section is called "Donations," but relatively few of the answers are found in ch. 10. It's also about notary practice and recordation. It's not unusual for the examiners to title their exam section in a way that raises that act in a scenario while many of the answers are found in a different chapter. The table of contents doesn't help much, if so.

Even the twist where the very next question changes the scenario dramatically is fairly common. They move the surface of your understanding of facts enough that you have to be nimble (circling the big change on the question may help, like "mortgage cancellation" here). Fortunately, there may also be an exam section answered mainly from one chapter, such as ch. 23 on car titles.

2. E is correct. A is incorrect in that there are alternative methods for a licensed financial institution to make a request, without using a notary (p. 299). B is wrong because only when the original mortgage was secured by a *paraphed* obligation does it need to be an authentic act (p. 298). C is wrong because the section in the study guide is all about making a request for cancellation (p. 297: procedure for cancellation requires formal request), as is this question; there doesn't seem to be some automatic procedure for the mortgagee even to send the promissory note (p. 298). D is wrong because all requests are signed by the requesting party (p. 297), while the original mortgage could've included the mortgagee (lender), p. 387, who doesn't have to sign this request (and even then, the requesting party is not necessarily a signator to the original); it's also not clear that the mortgagor (debtor) has the "duty" to do anything. E is best.

3. E is correct. C is correct because the notary may be fined $200 for each violation (p. 60). And A is correct because the notary is subject to suspension for cause, for violating laws governing exercise of notarial duties (pp. 52, 638), which includes the recording duty. But this kind of failure is not on the list of grounds for automatic suspension (B) found on p. 52, so "all of the above" (D) is wrong.

4. D is correct. With the land crossing two parishes, the donation (or any conveyance of an immovable) must be filed in both parishes, p. 585. That can't be done by just a True Copy made by the notary (E), p. 585, though BTW the parties could just execute a second original at the signing. C is wrong because it doesn't matter where it's *signed*; even the shorter filing deadlines in Orleans Parish, and a few other wrinkles on pp. 59-60, turn on where the immovable is located, not where the instrument is executed.

Note that the recording rule about two-parish property is suggested in the guide section on True Copies, but is expressly stated as to mortgages on p. 294. It's worth making a cross-reference (from p. 59), or index entry in your book to find it exam day ("recording, two-parish land," pp. 294, 585).

> Tactic: A and B are each true statements by themselves, because it *does* have to be filed there, and neither A nor B says "*only* in" that parish. So, they are both true. But with D encompassing both A and B, it is the best answer. Choose the most complete option, and in this case that's D.
>
> If the examiners gave only option A without B or D, you should pick A as technically true (unless it said "only," or unless they offer a better answer). You should not decoy yourself from the right answer technically even though you studied enough to know the best answer—one they didn't offer you—requires it to be filed in a second parish, too. They may well leave out the very best answer—that prepared students would expect—and make you pick among incomplete ones.
>
> It's a little like when they present you with a very flawed library document but the questions aren't about what's wrong with it, leaving the prepared students—ready to fix the problem—wondering what the real question is. Occasionally it's not a choice of the "best answer" so much as the "least worst" answer.

5. C is correct (as the one false option). Minors over 16 only have the capacity to donate inter vivos to their spouse or children (pp. 130-31); the minor can also leave things to someone other than spouse or kids by donation mortis causa (will). So, B and D are true. This age limitation is true even if the minor is emancipated by marriage (so C is false). A is wrong (is true) because even notaries with limited jurisdiction can file anywhere—they just can't *sign* outside their appropriate parish(es)—as nothing in App. A's rules about such notaries mentions location of registry.

> Tactic: when the set-up is "which is true?" or "which is false?" and you see two answers that seem to contradict each other (as arguably B and C do here), consider picking the answer from between those two only. That way, even if you're confused by another option (A is tough because it's about notary practice more than making copies, and deduced only from nothing in the book prohibiting older notaries from *filing* state-wide), you can often infer that the real battle is between the two answers most opposite of each other.

13 • ANSWERS TO EXAM C

6. A is correct. St. Charles Parish is not grouped with other parishes for reciprocal jurisdiction (B), p. 58. The map on p. 57 does show it next to Jefferson Parish, but also shows Jefferson has too many people to qualify for the "adjacent parish" rule on p. 57; so, C is wrong, and having an office there would not allow a signing without the dual commission status of A. But the notary may hold a dual commission in a second parish where they have an office open to the public (p. 68). They do have to post a second bond for a dual commission (so D is wrong), which is waived only if the adjacent parish has less than 40,000 people.

Note that the examiners occasionally do ask about pre-2005 notaries' limited jurisdiction and reciprocal parishes, even though it's irrelevant to the rules for someone passing their exam. Same with olographic wills and some other instruments which can't be done by a notary. Anything in the guide is fair game. It may seem odd that they'd test you on stuff you don't deal with, but especially when it contrasts with what you do handle—such as that limitation of usufruct terms can be done in a notarial will but not intestate—it makes sense to expect you to know it.

7. B is correct. Donations inter vivos must be immediate in their intention (even if its effective date is delayed because the donee puts off the written acceptance). In this instance, with all parties signing the document, it should have immediate effect (pp. 132, 382). The donor must understand he is losing his property *now*. This may qualify as some other act, such as a contract, but the question asks if the donation is valid, and it isn't. A is incorrect because it focuses on the (true) necessity of an express acceptance, but here that's not the problem (but it distracts because it states a true rule you learned—one that just doesn't address the problem of future donation). C is incorrect because it would be accepted when then the donee signs, and anyway putting off the effective date is the problem rather than a result. D is incorrect, or at least not as good as the emphatic B, in that it is an unclear and conditional explanation why the donation is invalid, implying that if the filing date could be met the donation would be fine. Here, it's possible the filing could be accomplished anyway, so that's not really the problem. It distracts because it gives a common sense reason why 14 days is an issue (less so outside of Orleans Parish, because recall the filing limit is 15 days in other parishes, p. 59), when in fact the immediacy rule is not about filing but is part of the basic concept of donation.

8. A is correct (as not needed). Tax ID information is usually related to a security interest (pp. 63, 340), such as a land sale with a mortgage—not a transfer without encumbrance (or debt). The other items B through D are all part of the content of act for a donation, found in ch. 21 at pp. 383-84 rather than ch. 10 on donations. You should write a visible cross-reference in ch. 10 that the content and form of the transfer—the act of donation—start at p. 383.

9. B is correct. Usufruct *is* a personal servitude, as A says (distracting you with a term that makes it seem like it can't transfer). But its interest may be alienated (i.e., transferred, including donation or sale, p. 101). D is wrong since usufructs end with the death of the usufrutary (p. 106), so it's not inheritable. C is wrong because the usufructuary may not donate the property itself, at least real property like this. That's suggested on p. 103, though you could be misled by the statement on p. 102, "when the usufructuary sells…" Certain property can be disposed of by the usufructuary, but real property and non-consumables may not be (at least when given inter vivos). That's made stark only on p. 484, so cross-reference to that page from p. 103—or write there the limitation when it's real property or non-consumables. (Technically, it's possible that the original creation of the usufruct was by testament, which could've provided that the usufructuary may alienate real property, but none of these facts are in the scenario and can't be assumed; so, B is "best" as an unconditionally true statement.)

Section 2

10. B is correct (as not really a problem). Though the example at the end of ch. 24 is mostly written from the point of view of the testator, there's nothing in the rest of the chapter to suggest that the introductory clauses such as the appearance cannot be written as many acts are, with the notary introducing the situation (it's a notarial testament) and the parties (appearance clause), such as with BEFORE ME... (And technically in all notarial testaments the required attestation clause is written not from the testator's perspective anyway.) The dispositive portion of the will is personal and would be written in the testator's first person. The larger issue that this is an affidavit rather than a testament relates vaguely to this point about "point of view," but still it's true that appropriate portions of a valid will may be the notary's story. A is true as a reason to invalidate the will, because there should be an attestation clause at the end, not a jurat—or at that exact spot it'd be the testator's conclusion of "This testament consisting of…" (p. 509). C violates the statutory directive of the notary's full name (p. 63), since initials are not enough (also pp. 336, 637). Likewise, the notary ID number is required (pp. 63, 637), at least here where there's no mention that a stamp or embosser added that. Failure of these name/number directives may not invalidate the will, but omitting here does violate R.S. 35:12.

> Tactic: note the "not" in the call of the question. It's easy to skip over those while reading the question, though obviously it is crucial. They may not help you out by capitalizing it (though they tend to). Generally, don't assume that the examiners will go out of their way to clear up double-negatives ("which is not an exception?") or emphasize key words ("which of the following is *false*?"). Not every question asks for the true answer, and you have to be on the lookout. Reading details in scenarios is crucial, too; they're unlikely to highlight the key phrase in it ("at the time of death," "appearing for the LLC," "both parties sign," etc.).
>
> If the set-up confuses you, simply circle, in the call of the question each time, "false," "true," "except," "not," and "invalid." That way the orientation of the question will stay fixed for you while you look through the answer options.

11. D is correct. Marital status may affect ownership of listed property (p. 340); at the least it's a required duty of the notary to include it (pp. 62, 337). Option A is incorrect because some juridical acts may be affidavits but nonetheless are authentic acts, such as affidavits of corrections, p. 634 (and with any affidavit there's no real prohibition against witnesses; they're just usually unnecessary and atypical). B is incorrect in that a will need not be comprehensive as to all the property; it can bequeath only part of the estate (p. 459). Even if a chunk of the estate isn't read as included in the listed legacies, it doesn't invalidate the will—that part is just treated as intestate (p. 459). E is wrong because appearances for a testament use residence (p. 507), unlike most other authentic acts that require domicile, pp. 336-37 (at least if recorded).

C is wrong but subtle, because you may recognize that parts of the 2018 will may not be revoked (see p. 505). Even if the 2018 will stands as not explicitly revoked, a legacy in the new will that is inconsistent with one in the 2018 will wouldn't make the new legacy invalid (the call of this question), but would revoke or modify the 2018 one (p. 507 note 5). So, even though the set-up says little about the terms of the 2018 will, it's not a reason to declare this will or its legacy invalid. And it's not a mandatory duty of the notary to revoke prior wills.

D is not a perfect answer, since it's true that not mentioning the marriage in itself doesn't render the will invalid (p. 507 note 6). Maybe it affects the legacy, but at the least it violates a requirement of law imposed on the notary. D raises the only issue that's overtly problematic with this will (of the options given).

12. *C is correct.* That Jan is deaf and 16 isn't an incapacity in her serving as a witness to a testament. There is an age cut-off for a will's witness (unlike to other acts), but 16 just qualifies (pp. 350, 476). B is a distractor because the guide says on both of those pages that deaf people cannot serve as witnesses—but then adds (in a way that's easy to miss) that this prohibition is for wills received under the provision for ones where the testator can't read. So, stated positively: deaf witnesses are fine as long as the testator isn't blind or illiterate. This question says Sandra read the will. A is wrong because there's no requirement for the 16-year-old to be found to be mature as such, but even if there were an issue of her "proper understanding," it's the notary that'd be the one to notice that, p. 498 (remember, AA are meant to be self-proving in court, pp. 319-21, not second-guessed easily there). D wrongly focuses on the age of someone to contract (p. 167) or donate inter vivos (pp. 130, 460), as opposed to *witness* age—but even a 16-year-old testator may make a valid will (pp. 459-60).

13. *D is correct.* There's no problem of Tommy being executor (C), because naming one is not a "legacy" (p. 477). As a witness, though, he can't enforce the legacy of the watch unless he would otherwise be an heir (pp. 476-77); but unrelated to Sandra, Tommy isn't. Still, the guide emphasizes—and they've tested on this—that the will itself is not invalid, just the witness's legacy (p. 477). So, neither A nor B is correct (nor E) because they say "Yes," the will is invalid.

14. *C is correct.* There's no general requirement (A) that signatures match the full name of any signer (p. 345). B is wrong because it broadly states that marks are OK for signing a will, but that would only be true for certain testators, and only then for notarial wills not olographic ones (pp. 345, 500). D is generally true for witnesses to acts, but not for the witness to a notarial will (p. 346). This question is hard because these rules are spread over three pages, and they're in ch. 19 on *signatures* generally rather than all being in the ch. 24 section on witnesses to a will. This recommends making a note on pp. 476 and 500 cross-referencing to pp. 344-46 and 350 (such as "signing by testator and witness—pp. 344-46, 350").

15. B is correct. This is the effect of having a grandchild born of a predeceased child who himself would be less than 24 at the time of decedent's death (pp. 479-80): representation occurs and the grandchild is treated as a forced heir. The amount of forced heirship when there's only one of them, as is true here, is 1/4 of the estate, or $30,000. A is wrong because, though the value is under the cap, the small succession procedure (for in-state actors, or ones like this with immovable property) is available only for *intestate* successions (p. 542). The question says the will is valid (and it doesn't become invalid just because a forced heir was not named in it—they just get their legitime [forced portion]), so this isn't a qualifying intestate situation. C is wrong because grandkids could be forced heirs, as noted above for this situation. D is wrong, both because Hugh is a successor in the *second* degree (pp. 448-49) and because there's no requirement that a valid testament leave more than the forced portion to relatives (pp. 479-80, 484); this option seems to be mixing up the intestate situation in which it would be true that Hugh, as the only descendant, would inherit everything (pp. 445-46). But the valid will precludes treating this as intestate.

> Tactic: it is odd to assume a will is valid when it is so fatally flawed at its inception (e.g., for being an affidavit rather than a will). But—if you're not asked about that, or in follow-up questions—take the examiners literally, assume it *is* valid, then examine the specific question asked. You don't want to get bogged down in the (understandable) thinking, "I can't salvage this so-called will, so none of the options make sense for this follow-up question." Or in this case, fall for the distractors of A and D, which would be closer to true if the will is invalid so the situation would be intestate.

16. D is correct. A is wrong because the small succession cut-off is $125,000 gross value of the estate (p. 542), here exceeded because there are two other items of property in the estate on the original will—one can assume gold coins have value. (Plus it's testate, so here that precludes small succession; see previous answer.) Power of attorney (C) doesn't make sense to transfer property of a deceased; who would even sign that? But B is a good distractor because in the abstract the scenario sounds like it's right for affidavit of heirship, used before a succession is opened. But that procedure is available to be signed by, and assign a vehicle to, heirs, legatees, or surviving spouse (p. 434), such as Ed and Craig. The form alone won't allow a non-relative to receive it this way. (One could argue that they could, in the process, donate it to Stu, but that would require an act of donation (p. 431) plus the nine other documents on pp. 434-35. Because the question (and choice E) speak of the form alone doing this, it's not right. Even if you don't see this fine print on p. 433, those nine other documents mean it's never going to be the form by itself that will make this happen.)

This question is hard not only because of the technicalities above but generally because the options are found in ch. 23 and ch. 27 rather than the wills chapter.

17. D is correct. When the present will was declared invalid, so was its value as an AA to revoke the December 2016 will (p. 479: citing a recent case, *Harlan*). So, the 2016 testament stands unrevoked because none of the methods of revoking or modifying a will (pp. 477-78, 484-85, 505) was validly used. (The facts don't mention any other effort to revoke the 2016 will, nor why the 2016 will didn't replace the 2013 one.) She didn't die intestate (C), and the 2013 will is not enforced (A). B is nearly true as far as it goes, but D is the best answer because it's more specific; in other words, B could mean either the 2013 or 2016 will, yet we know it's not the 2013 one. The only answer unconditionally true is D. (B is technically false for the reason that it leaves property to "heirs," but even if it said "legatees," it's not "best.")

18. A is correct. Mere preference or wishes are not enough to declare donative intent (pp. 501-02), at least for this particular legacy (it doesn't invalidate the will). B is wrong because a testator in a valid will can redirect property away from relatives in the first degree (p. 483), limited only by forced heirship (which doesn't seem relevant here). And in fact may give to non-family (p. 484). D is wrong because even if forced heirship does apply and limit the donation to a nephew, the precatory (mushy) words of "preference" invalidate this legacy. C is a true statement if this had an otherwise valid phrasing: stocks *are* incorporeal movables and coins *are* corporeal movables, and they may be bequeathed in a testament, but they aren't really "given" by mushy statements of desire.

19. C is correct. Successions law already accounts for the possibility that a spouse is named as a legatee or appointed in a role (here, executor) while still in an intact marriage, but is divorced from the deceased at the time of death. Remember it as being a rule of common sense. Unless the will provides for the spouse to continue even in the event of divorce (nothing here suggests that), the appointment and legacy are treated as invalid after divorce (pp. 485, 505 [item 5]). The will is otherwise valid. Note that this rule is found in the sections about Revocation rather than Executor. It's a rule that auto-revokes the legacy or appointment of a divorced spouse, but it's hard to find in the chapter unless you cross-reference.

20. A is correct (p. 445). This is a fairly common question on the official exam: making you identify the situation and named parties for a valid testament (testate/legatee) or for a deceased with no will (intestate/heir). It's just definitional but consider it low-hanging fruit that you don't want to miss. They may also do this kind of name-the-party format with mortgagor/mortgagee and in the process make you identify it as a conventional mortgage vs. a collateral one—and even though technically a collateral one is considered one form of conventional mortgage, it's the "best" answer between the two if the scenario is actually a collateral one, because it's the more precise answer.

> Tactic: don't read additional, unnecessary facts into the scenario. This question would seem to be more complicated if Ed has siblings, or other heirs are closer in degree. Then it's more accurate to say he is "an heir" rather than "the." But choice A is still true regardless, and certainly the best answer of the four.

Section 3

21. D is correct. The use of *venue* for a juridical act prepared by the notary (p. 332) relates to the signing location. But whether it's clear or not, that study guide mention isn't about the venue clause used on the similar-looking caption in a *court* filing—which is where it's filed, not signed. That should be left up to the attorney to fill in where the pleading or court paper will be filed. Non-attorney notaries just add them to stuff we create and sign, but we don't typically create court filings as such, e.g., pp. 318, 546. (Even affidavits are often attached to court filings, not filed separately as here.)

In this case, even without intuiting that different sense of venue clauses, the uncertainty over where to file should give the notary pause about filling in the blank—especially since as a lawyer's *strategy* it may be the unauthorized practice of law to decide where to file. A is the distractor because it's where the filing is signed; it's a strong (but wrong) decoy because the book's insistence that "venue" is "where the act is executed" (p. 332). Sure, for notarial acts that stand alone. BTW, even if the notary is also a lawyer (and you should not over-read that into the set-up), she is not acting in that role here, so that doesn't change the concern that it's not her job to fill in the blank.

22. C is correct. That's where the jurat goes. See p. 359 and an example on p. 587. Jurat is defined on p. 589. The distractor is A because its stated clause *is* found in an affidavit, but it goes after the appearance. B and D are not parts of affidavits. They could ask this question using actual phrases as options ("Sworn to and subscribed...") rather than the labels for them. Or give you an affidavit with a blank line for where the jurat should go, then ask you what words go in it. The August 2020 and January 2022 exams had several questions (considered difficult) that tested your knowledge of key phrases of appearance, conclusion, and signature used for various acts.

23. B is correct. This is done by a declaration of immobilization (p. 88). It must be authentic as a standalone act not part of a sale or mortgage instrument (pp. 324, 385). It could possibly (even probably) be made in affidavit form (A), but nothing in the guide's description of this declaration says that it *must* be or that would be enough (pp. 86, 88). Certainly this answer is not "best" compared to B. Options C and D are wrong in allowing a process less than authentic act. This question is difficult even though it's right out of the guide because it's hard to locate in it unless you followed the lead of "component parts" (it's a page after that term's defined), or indexed it. It's also hard because the page discussing this kind of declaration doesn't say it has to be AA (at least in the context of a mobile home); that's found on the list of AA-required acts on p. 324 (which itself doesn't explain immobilization in terms of "components part"). You should write "pp. 88, 385" next to its related entry on p. 324, and make a note on p. 88 that the declaration may have to be AA (there, referencing to p. 324). This question, like many formats they ask nowadays, makes you piece together parts of the book unless you already know that turning it into a component part is an act of immobilization.

24. C is correct. The notary's "seal" is her signature, so no stamp or embosser is required (p. 74). Though some places won't recognize this to be true, a Louisiana court would know the law (so B is wrong). A is wrong because it is not John's signature alone that makes it a valid affidavit; even if this option is read as meaning John's signature as notarized, it's not "best" compared to C, which is a firm statement of the rule. D is wrong because Nancy's state-wide jurisdiction from taking the state exam (p. 58) means that she *can* execute an affidavit outside her home parish of commission; the language about oaths being state-wide applies to pre-2005 notaries (see pp. 56, 634), whereas everything is state-wide to a notary commissioned June 2005 or later (p. 58). So, D is a true statement of a rule that doesn't apply to these facts, just to pre-2005 notaries.

25. A is correct. The methods of establishing identity of a signator are on pp. 74 and 334-35. Here, Nancy has known John a long time (even less time would be fine as long as the notary can reasonably fix identity by personal knowledge). B through D are not required here, and D is wrong in suggesting a school ID would suffice.

26. C is correct, as seen at the same study guide section (pp. 74-75). Someone personally known to the notary may then identify a signator in such a way that the signator need not show ID. The warning at p. 75 is about a case in which the person vouching for the signator wasn't *known* to the notary, who's just going off of ID for the vouching party. But this is a case where the notary knows John. A and B are wrong in making the voucher's ID suffice. D is wrong in making the rule of vouching turn on the voucher being a signator, too, which is not what the rule is about; it's a rule about identifying a signer, not of co-signing. There's no issue generally about identifying signers based on whether they're signing one or two documents, nor a rule that allows vouching 'more easily' for joint documents.

27. D is correct. Our job is to administer a serious process of oath and signing, not to check the truth of the affidavit's assertions of fact (see p. 76). We do have a duty of establishing basic capacity (p. 317), as A says, but that is not about the issue here: whether we attest to the truth of others' sworn statements. B is wrong in that, even though it's true that the affidavit is personal to the affiant (pp. 331, 365), that rule is at most a vague justification for not vouching for contents; D is "best" because it's specific and supported by a rule suggested by the study guide. C is wrong because, while it's true that testaments and other authentic acts assume a process of review and verifying understanding (see pp. 320-21, 629-30), that's not true for the contents of an affidavit (except perhaps for the few that are also authentic, but even then the notary is not verifying the affiant's "truths").

28. B is correct. The only valid signature is one made in front of you (e.g., p. 608). A is incorrect because sending an ID with someone doesn't mean the person on the ID is signing in front of the notary (no matter how well known the one bringing the ID is). C is wrong because the rule of vouching for another's identity (pp. 74-75) doesn't authorize trusting the person with saying the *signature* is hers. D is wrong because sending a witness of the initial signature to sign an acknowledgment isn't allowed to verify an affidavit (pp. 328, 331). This question may seem too easy, because it's basic that the signings are done before you, not at home—but in fact it has been used before, with their wrinkle being trusting a childhood friend. Take the low-hanging fruit and don't overthink this (e.g., D's witness acknowledgment method that distracts but is wrong for an affidavit).

Section 4

29. B is correct. This is a classic example of metes and bounds (pp. 407-12). Part of the description does show (part of) a section of a township, so C sounds to be technically true. But B is the best answer because the statement as a whole is in metes and bounds form, not just a small part of it. Choose the more complete, comprehensive answer. Another reason why C is less-good is that a literal "section of a township" is much bigger than this described portion of it. Note that when they do ask questions about property descriptions out of ch. 22, a common form is asking what kind of description it is.

30. A is correct. In a metes and bounds description, "commencing point" is a fixed location [here, that NE corner] to start tracking **to** the actual tract being described, at which place [here, the plaque] the "point of beginning" is named (p. 408). Commencing point = point of beginning if the property begins *at* the fixed spot; so, the distractor is that there are examples in the guide which suggest the point of beginning *is* the commencing point (pp. 409, 411), making D tempting. But for *this* one, they are different. The plaque may serve as the original bearing in some sense, but "point of beginning" is a term of art and "original bearing" is not. Use the legally significant term if it's given as an option, not a paraphrase.

31. C is correct (as false). The tract is part of the township but does not "encompass" it, or occupy it completely. It's just a part. It is true, as A says, that the correct term in the blank determines closing the land (p. 410). And that term here is "point of beginning," so B is true that "commencing point" makes it flawed, by *not* closing the land (because in this example, unlike some in the guide, the point of beginning is not the same as the commencing point—so you can only close the land at the plaque where the actual tract begins). D is true that it's common (modern) practice to include the "improvements" language after the blank (p. 379). BTW, don't be distracted if it's called the "point of commencement" instead of "commencing point," as those are used interchangeably in ch. 22 (whereas "point of beginning" may be distinct, as in this scenario).

13 • ANSWERS TO EXAM C

32. A is correct. This description is in the form of a subdivision and describes a lot in the subdivision (pp. 412-13). It's not closing the land, as in B (p. 410); not in the form of per aversionem, C (p. 406); and not metes and bounds, D (p. 407).

33. D is correct. Without the "improvements" language at the end, it's possible that this would be read as selling the land underneath the house or other such "improvements" to land (p. 404). A is wrong, or not "best," because it's not necessarily part of a mortgage—lots of acts besides mortgages have a property description in them; and leaving out this particular language doesn't affect having a mortgage or not. Similarly, B is wrong because it's not about a donation either (though again a donation could include a description); anyway, it's not about whether it's authentic either. C is wrong because it conveys only Lot 21 of the subdivision, and anyway it's not what's missing here. You'd need to look at a typical subdivision description (pp. 412-13) to tell what's missing.

34. C. is correct. A paraph is a way for a notary to connect an instrument to a supporting document (p. 595). It's used a lot to link mortgages with promissory notes (p. 391), but that's not its only use (p. 595). The paraph itself could go on the description while the recitation of paraph would then go on the legal instrument (the act of donation, the cash sale, etc.). Beware ever using it in a will, though incorporation by reference to a property description may be allowed (p. 503). D is the distractor but really means an act that sets up a corporation, even though the larger subject here is "incorporating" an external document (p. 360); one wouldn't describe a form or clause for incorporating it as an "act" in any event. Option A, despite sounding right, is wrong because "unincorporated association" is a type of business entity (p. 571). B is wrong because "jurat" is for affidavits.

Anyway, this doesn't usually *have* to be done with a paraph, as the form used on p. 360 would do (then attaching the property description). But recitation of paraph on the instrument is the best answer given and is certainly an available way to link the two documents together. You may want to write cross-references on pp. 391 and 595 because full info on other uses of a paraph is on p. 595.

Section 5

35. C is correct. This is a limited emancipation by authentic act (pp. 192-93, 589-90). The other instruments do entirely different things, though one could confuse power of attorney (A) in that it is also a document that empowers someone to do something. But here, Susan is not empowering him to act *for her*, as with a power of attorney.

Note that the heading for this group of questions could be "Limited Emancipation," but that would give away too much. The examiners may want you to find the act that provides a solution, as this question does. The group does involve an LLC in places, but most of the answers won't be found in ch. 28 on businesses.

36. A is correct because this act must be in authentic form (pp. 192, 589) and is on the AA list at p. 324. He isn't emancipated *in any way* with this invalid act.

B is wrong because it focuses on whether the authorized actions need be AA (and it's true these two don't), making it confuse the rule that powers of attorney don't have to be AA if they are used for acts that themselves aren't AA (p. 250)—but this is a limited emancipation, not a power of attorney. C is wrong because the setting up of an LLC is not an AA; but even if it were, that's a very limited statement, implying that the act could be used for some purposes. D is wrong because it must be an AA.

Note that D is wrong for an additional reason: even if were an AA, its authorization would be limited to acts that are authorized, not just any act an 18-year-old could do.

> Tactic: an official question may not be so clear in saying he is single (we've made it a bit easier by assuming away that complication). Still, don't read the extra fact into this scenario that he might be married and already emancipated. The most natural reading of the facts, that they are trying to authorize his actions, would not be needed if he's married.

37. D is correct (as false) because he doesn't have to be 18 to execute a valid will (p. 460), though for any testator their capacity is also a function of their general comprehension of the consequences of the act (p. 460), as B says. Susan's instrument doesn't change that one way or the other, since the age requirement for writing a will is stated in terms of years, not that someone is treated legally as a major. She probably wouldn't have the authority to change the age rule for him (any more than she could emancipate him to vote at age 17), but that's not how the question is framed. A is true (so it's wrong) because acts of emancipation are limited exactly that way (pp. 589-90). It's not allowed, no matter how expressly stated. C is a correct statement of the rule for powers of attorney (p. 251), even though this instrument is not a POA. (Admittedly it doesn't directly apply to this situation, which involves emancipation, so it'd be a false answer if the option were framed in terms of this *being* a POA or a reason why it's invalid, instead of as a broader, true statement of a rule.)

> Tactic: this answer cannot be found just in the two sections on emancipation in ch. 12 and 29. The 'capacity for a testament' aspect is found in ch. 10 or 24. Option C's rule about testaments and mandates is in ch. 15. The actual exam will have several questions that have an answer straight out of the study guide, but finding it in the right place puts a premium on cross-referencing beyond what the authors provide, or indexing it by inserting entries into the glossary pages.

38. B is correct. Ending or modifying the emancipation (here, modifying it) is not effective against third parties until filed for registry (*where* depends on im-movables vs. movables), as seen on pp. 193 and 590. But the original act need not be filed (p. 192); that's one of the few instances in the book where an act is valid against third parties at signing rather than filing. Option A is a bit of a distractor, in that you probably would file them in the same place if you decided to file the original, but it implies you must have done that—or at the least is not "best" compared to B, which is an unqualified true statement consistent with pp. 192-93 and 589-90 (and those pages show why C and D are wrong). The mention of Acadia Parish may be a distractor, or an added layer of reading comprehension, because while that's not the problem here with any answer, it's true that filing to affect movables is in the parish where the minor is domiciled (pp. 193, 590).

39. C is correct because liability for damages is not waivable in a notarial *act* of limited emancipation (p. 590), just by other methods of emancipation. A is wrong because the instrument doesn't itself form an LLC (a process explained in ch. 28), yet even if John forms one as he is authorized here to do—but don't read that step into the scenario—it might protect John, and possibly not Susan. B is wrong because even an express waiver of this type is ineffective against such claims. D is wrong because it focuses on filing. While often registry of an instrument is required before it affects third parties (e.g., p. 39), it's not needed for the original act of emancipation (#38 above). But this choice suggests it would be effective to waive liability had it been filed, which is not true anyway.

If you didn't really understand "liability for damages" when you saw that in the state study guide, it's mainly about tort law: it's having to pay for "personal injury," which can be more than just accidents with physical damage. ("Torts" is French for "wrongs.") In Louisiana, unlike any other state, parents are vicariously liable for their kids (gulp), except after other forms of emancipation than the notarial one. This means if the child commits a tort or causes damages by breach of contract, the parent must pay for it even if the parent isn't at fault. Don't get distracted by the phrase "errors and omissions" in the question, as it has nothing to do with the E&O policy you may buy as a notary (p. 65) except E&O protects against malpractice, too. Remember that a "tort" sounds delicious but it isn't— and if your kid makes one, you clean the kitchen mess.

14

Answers and Explanations: Mini-Exam D

Section 1

1. A is correct. The answer is a combination of two different rules OMV uses to "name" people who get a certificate of title: (1) the suffix "Sr." is not included, since it is not part of the legal name on their birth certificate; (2) the only punctuation allowed is hyphen and ampersand (*Fundamentals* (2022), p. 438), so not periods or apostrophes here. (Since spaces in last names don't count either, I tell my students to remember that St. Andalone comes out as STANDALONE.)

> Tactic: don't fight the ordinary facts suggested by the scenario. Sure, you could imagine a scenario where a "Sr." legally changes his name to include that after Junior is born. Then presumably OMV would allow it. But that's not usual and should not be over-read into the factual set-up here. Such an odd twist is not mentioned in the facts, so don't imagine it *could* be there, answering as if it is.

2. C is correct (as the one method of "endorsement" *not* allowed). See p. 424. The buyer doesn't have to sign it before the notary, just the seller does. (That makes sense, because we worry about the buyer grifting a car by forging the seller's name, not vice versa.) A and B both cover that important requirement. C doesn't actually say that the notary sees the seller sign it, so it's not proper endorsement. D is a proper alternative to having the seller sign in front of the notary: use witness acknowledgment (pp. 424-25).

3. E is correct. Odometer disclosure (A) would be required today for most cars model year 2011 or later (p. 434); but this is a 2009 car, and "is obtaining" is present tense (take tense seriously on the notary exam!). Bill of sale (B) is not essential for typical in-state transfers that don't raise tax implications (pp. 430-31). Power of attorney (C), discussed at p. 435, is easily not needed for ordinary transfers where the seller can just sign, as here; it has its place in more complex situations (e.g., if there are co-owners of the car selling it, but only one can go to this notary—then the other needs to use another notary ahead of time to empower the second to sign the title for both of them before a notary). Power of attorney is so far from the scenario facts given that D becomes a tempting distractor, as at least A and B would make sense as documentation you certainly *could* add, consistent with the scenario. But here, neither is "required."

4. D is correct (as false). B is true: at least for this kind of private transaction not involving a licensed car dealer, the OMV won't issue a new certificate of title without a valid donation by authentic act (AA), as explained on pp. 152 and 431 (and on other pages, so it seems testable). But A is also true: even without getting the title, ownership does transfer with a valid donation made as a manual gift (e.g., physical delivery) and acceptance, even without an AA (pp. 148, 431). C is true because it doesn't *have* to be a manual gift as in option A, as the transfer is complete with the AA and acceptance, even without delivery (p. 146). A is the trickiest: you'd think if the OMV is requiring an AA (however it gets accepted by donee), then donee doesn't own the car without one. But actually one can legally own the car, if not get new title to it, by manual gift rather than AA. D is therefore false, and the "right" answer.

5. D is correct. One of the methods to make separate property into community is to transfer it into the community by a stipulation made as an AA (pp. 133-34, 205). It can be done as a writing by onerous title, but where, as here, it's gratuitous (the set-up makes clear there's no strings attached), it must be AA much like a donation. A is wrong because it can easily be community without getting the OMV involved and issuing a title; lots of property with one spouse's name on the title is community (e.g., p. 204, discussing how one spouse can manage community property registered just in their name). B is wrong because it was not community when Roy received it as a donation just to himself (p. 204). C describes one way that Roy could donate it to Tina as a manual gift without an AA (pp. 148, 431), but that would result in Tina owning the car—not making it community with each having a half-interest. That result wasn't Roy's stated goal.

Section 2

6. B is correct (as ineffective to empower Bart to handle the deal). That act would be an effort to acquire things with separate funds and keep them out of the community (p. 204), so it has no use in this transaction. A power of attorney expressly appointing Bart as her agent/attorney-in-fact in the sale would work (pp. 247, 251), either in the form of a procuration (A) or a mandate (D). C is true, too, because Amy could renounce her right to concur, in writing (p. 202), allowing Bart to unilaterally alienate their community condo.

7. D is correct. Items of modest value compared to the "economic position" of the spouses, even if community, can be donated by one spouse without concurrence by the other (pp. 133-34, 203), at least if it's a "usual or customary gift." That may describe this gift, at least well enough to be the best answer. A is wrong since typically furniture in the family home *is* the kind of community property that requires concurrence; it's a relative nullity without it (p. 202). B and C are wrong since the transfer didn't fail in its inception, for that "customary gift" reason. FWIW, C is more wrong, since it's certainly not an *absolute* nullity (p. 202).

> Tactic: it's tempting when two answers seem very similar except for one key difference (relative vs. absolute) to assume the correct choice reduces to one of those two. But it's possible, like here, that the thing they *share* (null) is wrong.

8. A is correct. Donation can be accomplished without an AA if it's a corporeal movable (like a sofa) and it's a manual gift (p. 148). That happened when it was delivered to her (she picked it up—don't get locked into the idea that "delivered" means *he* has to drive it over to her; in any event, she's possessing it). B is incorrect as the opposite of the rule: it's true that this gift is neither onerous nor remunerative (the rest of option B makes clear it's gratuitous), but then that'd mean that it *would* need an AA if it didn't otherwise fall into the manual gift rule of choice A (p. 146). C is wrong because this is not an *incorporeal* movable subject to that (correctly stated) exception on pp. 148-49. You'd have to know the difference between incorporeal and corporeal things, from ch. 8 (p. 87). D is similarly wrong because, if it really is a donation in disguise (though no facts suggest a disguise), that'd just mean it *would* be required to be an AA (p. 147).

9. B is correct. Transfer of separate property (this house) into the community ("legal regime") must be done by AA, if it's gratuitous (pp. 133-34, 205). The "no conditions" language assures you it's gratuitous. Transfer by onerous title (with conditions) would only need to be in writing, as in C, but this one's gratuitous. This rule also applies to movables (#5 above). "Juridical act" in A may describe an act that is not necessarily authentic (see definition given on p. 315), so it's not enough. D is wrong because there's nothing on pp. 133 or 205 that requires Bart to be part of the act at that time. D is also not "best" compared to B because B contains the important qualifier that makes this act gratuitous.

> Tactic: this works like a donation, but your exam may call it a "transfer." If so, note that gratuitous transfer of this interest is on the p. 324 magic list of AA-required acts. If a scenario like this is stated in terms of a "donation," that's more generally in ch. 10, especially p. 146 saying gratuitous donations are AA. Maybe write next to that spot a cross-reference to p. 133 noting "transfer of SP → CP." And write "AA" in the margins of pp. 133 and 205 so that you don't only get that requirement from p. 324. To make the question harder, they may make such a transfer of SP interest either onerous or remunerative, in which case AA is not required (unless the value of the compensation or condition is less than 2/3 of the SP interest's value [compare p. 150]).

10. D is correct. Recordation goes in the parish where the immovable property is located and—because the jewelry and clothes are movables—*also* where the couple's domicile is (pp. 209, 591). They haven't yet moved to Jeff Parish so it'd seem that East Baton Rouge would be included, as their domicile. This isn't about state marriage records (even then, marriage certificates start in the parish), so B is wrong. A and C are incomplete in that they don't have filing in the other parish, too.

Note some ambiguity on p. 591 about the place of recordation if the agreement just involves an immovable. The *text* of p. 591 says that recordation goes in the parish where property is located *and* where the couple's domicile is. In this example that would be East Baton Rouge and Jefferson. But really it's more clearly stated at p. 209 that, for immovables, you file where it's situated (here, you wouldn't need to file in East Baton Rouge too, if no movables); and that's more consistent with the code article 2332 quoted at p. 591 too (below the text summary). To be sure the text doesn't make you stumble on exam day, write a "?" and arrow on p. 591 at "and," forcing you to read the statute following, which separates immovables from movables. In our question, adding movables like jewelry papers over this confusion: filing in *both* parishes is now required.

11. B is correct. See p. 208 and especially the fuller discussion on p. 326. It is true that the matrimonial agreement may be executed either through AA or by "act under private signature duly acknowledged," so answer A is generally true. But the call of this question is about *when* it's valid. For the acknowledgment method, that's when the acknowledgment is signed before a notary, not when the couple originally signs. So A is incorrect the way the question is presented here. Certainly a notarized agreement without witnesses at some point (C) is not enough. It is doubtful that a mere affidavit (D) would contain the component parts of a valid marriage agreement (see p. 591), but at any rate option D doesn't mention there are witnesses, which at least the acknowledgment alternative has at some point in time.

Note also the very testable 2017 case on p. 208 saying that signing before the ceremony is not enough if acknowledged after, which applies the timing rule emphasized for marital agreements on p. 326. But it's not mentioned in the Matrimonial Agreement section in ch. 29, so perhaps on p. 590 note a reference like "timing of signatures if not AA, see pp. 208-09, 326." This is not just about when it becomes effective; the act itself is not *valid* if it wasn't acknowledged before the marriage, even if the parties go to a notary and acknowledge it after.

Section 3

12. C is correct. It would also be correct if it said "credit sale" or "act of sale with vendor's lien." They're all the same whatever the label: owner-financed sale of an immovable (p. 368). That's exactly what's happening in this deal.

13. A is correct (as the one *not* needed in the act). The due-on-sale clause is not about protecting the mortgagee in the event of non-payment, and does not allow fast-track foreclosure. It's about accelerating payments if you sell the place (p. 373). The others listed are all normal requirements for a mortgage (or, like here, owner-financing much like a mortgage though not from a third party like a bank). See pp. 370-71, 385. The examiners often give a mortgage, donation, or sale of an immovable then ask you what content does or doesn't have to be included in that act. Social security last-4 (B) is interesting because it's only needed for financing docs like this, not cash sales or donations (any more). C is true because of the confession of judgment clause: that's when you must make a mortgage (or credit sale like this) an AA (pp. 389-90).

Tactic: make a list, somewhere handy in the study guide, of the situations which require social security info. There aren't that many, yet they get tested precisely because they are so targeted to those contexts but are not pervasively required. See *Sidepiece* (2022), p. 95, for this and other such lists.

14. C is correct; that's a classic situation to use *dation* (pp. 151 and 379-81). The other answers are also found in ch. 21 on conveyances, but don't have this effect of release of the remaining obligation. D is wrong, even if this feels like a "return" to John, because the right of redemption would have to be set up that way at the initial transfer, not something done eight years later. Distractor E sounds like it could be right, because Helen's giving up her claim, "quitting" it, but quitclaim is a term of art that doesn't fit this kind of forgiveness of debt for transfer of a known ownership interest (not a possible-maybe one, like the quitclaim normally has). Even if you *could* do this through quitclaim (and maybe a separate agreement striking the debt), it's certainly not the best answer compared to the by-definition one, C.

Tactic: it is common on the state exam to have a question asking you to categorize the "form of conveyance" from a set of ambiguous scenario facts. (I doubt they'd have *three* as straightforward as this, the next, *and* #12.). Make sure you go into the exam knowing the essential differences for every heading of ch. 21. You can use the detailed table-of-contents as a checklist of them (pp. xxii-xxiii), to test yourself. Also, know the difference between a *dation* and donations (see p. 151).

15. A is correct. It's a straightforward bond-for-deed, p. 372, which is a contract *to* sell (someday) rather than a contract *that sells* (now). The guide makes clear (p. 372) this is "not a true credit sale" (B). Note the very strict requirements for using a bond-for-deed contract when there's a mortgage (pp. 372-73), and the fact that such a contract may trigger a due-on-sale clause (p. 373).

16. B is correct. As a contract, rather than a transfer of title as such (see p. 372), there wouldn't seem to be a need between the parties to record the act. But the book makes clear that, to affect third parties, such contracts are required to be registered (p. 373). Thus, A and C are wrong even though most of the other conveyances in ch. 21 must be filed (and A is further wrong in stating that it conveys the property). D is almost correct, in that the bond-for-deed doesn't necessarily culminate in the transfer of property, and doesn't do that immediately, but it's meant to obligate the seller eventually ("culminate") to deliver title to the buyer. Even if one interprets "culminate" as the contract, rather than the ultimate goal of the arrangement, B is the best answer, as more precise and straightforward, and itself found in the study guide.

17. C is correct. A valid testament need not include a legal property description (e.g., p. 507). It is clear that donation inter vivos, in A (p. 383); act of sale, B (p. 367); and sale with right of redemption, D (p. 377) all require a full property description in their content of act (or incorporated by reference, p. 360).

18. B is correct. A is wrong because the prohibition against donating all you own is for donations inter vivos (pp. 137-38). In fact, most testaments donate everything (though they don't *have* to, p. 459). So, this is an appropriate situation for such a complete disposition. C is wrong because, though donations are subject to forced heirship and part of his estate would be called the "disposable portion" (p. 479), this disposition doesn't violate any such limit: he's giving his disposable part and the forced part to the same person, his only heir of the first degree. D is wrong because he doesn't have to reserve a usufruct to Jane, in his valid testament (pp. 483-84).

15

Exam Strategies*

Exam Format and Test-taking Tips

The usual format is 72 to 80 questions, all multiple choice. Typically, there are four options to choose from, or occasionally five—and not two, or true-false as such. It is possible that some questions will be worded in terms of true-false options, but still leaving four choices for you to discern. For example, after a statement of facts or reference to a scenario or its library, the call of the question may be something like: "Which of the following [four] statements is false?"

One format they've used makes choice D as "None of the above" or "All of the above." Yet the set-up to all questions (in bold face at the top of the exam) is to choose the "best answer." In exam-creation, it is not normally considered best practice to combine the general "best answer" instruction with a specific question that includes "None of the above," because there may be some reason that one of the other choices is not perfect but the others are very wrong—so, is "none" the best choice, or the imperfect but better option among the other two?

Or the general instruction confuses you with "D. All of the above," because you may believe that one of the options in A through C is clearly better than the other two. So the best answer might be, say, C. But none is actually wrong. Do you choose C as "best" or is "all" in fact best?

My best advice is that if the first three options are all wrong, even for some technical or picky reason, choose "D. None of the above," even though some are way more wrong than others. But if there's a fair case to be made that one answer is barely correct, if imperfectly stated, choose it rather than "none." And for "All of the above," use it even if one answer is not great. The good news is that they're likely to offer "all" in a situation where you can already tell that two of the options are correct. If you're right about that, it doesn't matter that you can think of a way to read the third choice as wrong; pick D.

Fortunately they don't use the "all" or "none" options too often in one administration. Hopefully, if they do, it will be pretty clear what they want you to pick as the right answer, assuming you know the information tested or can find it in the study guide.

As suggested above, some questions are worded in a globally positive or negative way, such as: Which of the following statements is *false*? This format tests your

---

* Excerpted and adapted from Childress, *Louisiana Notary Exam Sidepiece to the 2022 Study Guide*, ch. 4 and 5 (Quid Pro Books, © 2022).

ability to know (or find) choices from several places in the book, because the options don't have to be related in subject matter to each other. It may help to write "T" at the end of each option you think is true, reducing the options to the likely false one, because under test pressure it's easy to quickly mark the first statement that you're confident is correct—forgetting that you're supposed to pick the *false* one. I made that mistake on some practice exams until I made myself write "true" and "false" next to each option A through D, then went back to the call of the question above that to remind myself they're asking for the false one. And similarly where the call of the question is: Which of the following statements is true?

Even outside the true-false format with four options, many questions force you to use two or more different places in the book to answer the question as a whole. They can do this by breaking down the information *in the book* over two places; an example is the useful samples they give for appearances, split between pp. 338-39 and 354-57. Or the question itself makes you relate together two different rules to merge into one answer (say, the small succession can be in the form of an affidavit; affidavits can't be done via power of attorney; therefore, answer C is wrong because it's having an agent sign for one of the heirs using the succession-by-affidavit format). Either way, study and mark up the book in such a way that you can quickly go to multiple pages, to read the right answer or to merge two ideas into one right answer.

Scenarios and Standalone Questions

The Secretary of State site makes it sound like *all* the questions are based on "scenarios" (fact patterns of people doing things) which in turn rely on "libraries" of incomplete or incorrect forms. To be sure, they've moved in that direction more than in many years past. But the website's emphasis on this format obscures the fact that 15 or so of the questions are likely to be unconnected to any scenario or library of paperwork. They are straightforward questions about your knowledge of notary practice; Louisiana law in covered areas like property; court structure and jurisdiction; acts not supplied in a library; property descriptions, the civil law system; or even Louisiana history and geography related to the civil law.

These are standalone questions (rather than, elsewhere in the exam, a series of 10 to 15 based on one fact pattern). They are much like the legacy general-knowledge questions they used to test in a closed-book format. So you can't ignore the study guide's introductory ch. 1-7 just because it'd be hard to test these subjects via a scenario. Be happy these are in reality low-hanging fruit if you can recall the right answer (e.g., that the signature is your "seal," p. 74) or, easier still, just know enough to locate and confirm the right answer that's virtually quoted for you in the guide. The exam would be harder if they meant it when they suggest every question derives from a complicated fact pattern.

Even when the questions *are* based on a scenario, and part of the group of 10 or so questions tested "under" that scenario, it's sometimes the case that a particular question is only *loosely* based on the scenario—that the latter is just a jumping-off point to get you to define a term or apply a rule in a way that could've easily been asked without reference to the scenario. These feel like the scenario is more of an excuse to ask the question than a necessary part of it.

So it may be that, along with the low-hanging ones noted above, fully 15-20 of the actual questions (out of, say, 80) are pretty much standalone knowledge questions rather than analyze-the-scenario ones—despite the SOS website's description. That doesn't mean they're easy questions, or all just trivia. But they can be approached in a straightforward way, especially using good indexing and cross-referencing strategies with the study guide.

The scenario-based questions, too, make you use your ability to find relevant passages in the guide and apply them to the inquiry at hand—here, in the form of a fact pattern or library of sample documents. *Recognizing* the issue raised by the fact pattern, and the type of form that is being referenced in the library, is a crucial skill. The answer ultimately will be found somewhere in the guide, but you won't know where to look, even if you create an index, if you don't "get" the question and identify the issue.

The Forest and the Trees

You have to see the big picture and understand concepts cold to be able to look in the right place—even to know what table-of-contents or index term to look up. So, this puts a premium on using the book and any prep course you take to *conceptualize* notary law and forms. For example, knowing what a personal servitude is, and that there are other types besides usufructs (though that's the main one), is more important than knowing their detailed differences, assuming you can locate the differences quickly despite test pressure. That changes the way you study for the test from how it used to be administered a few years ago.

When it was an exam of memorization, code-article identification, and form-writing, there were a lot of details to learn by heart. There's still a lot of that involved in the current administration. But you can study each page knowing that specific details they can test—for instance, that property records have to be filed in Orleans Parish within 48 hours, unlike the 15 days elsewhere (pp. 59-60); or that there are only eight reasons you can disinherit a kid (p. 490)—need only be learned enough to see there's an issue (if Orleans is mentioned in the question for recordation, that means something; if a reason is given for disinheriting a kid, you know it's got to be on the statutory list). If you can find the right spot in the guide, the tiny *detail* they're testing (say, this deed was filed too late for Orleans; a daughter in the military hasn't talked to testator in years, but that doesn't let him cut her out of the will) can be answered during the exam.

There's still a lot of memorization necessary, but it's about learning the framework and general terms well, which is simply a different approach from what worked in years past. Study time is better spent learning the forest and projected subjects they test—and making the book into a ready reference—than in quizzing yourself on the eight reasons for disinherison, or the seven instruments that require a social security number. Turning the book into the reference resource is time-consuming, and offers no promise of less work, but the point is that the time marking up your book in an engaged way is more productive than flashcards, memory drills, and note-taking outside the confines of the study guide. Yes, it takes effort to annotate the guide with a list of the seven social-security-number situations; but you know if one comes up on the exam, and you've trained yourself to *recognize* the situation, you'll *find* their answer in the guide.

Thus, the format of the exam and its questions affects your study style and need to make locatable notes in the book.

Making Notes in Your Study Guide

However you write in the guide, the goal should be just enough information that you can *remember* broad concepts, organization, and key points from the notes, then *find* details and rules the day of the test as needed, as explained below. The student with the *most* notes won't necessarily be the winner. Even so, your judicious use of bullet-points and sample forms and acts may require more surface room than the book offers on its own, so it makes sense to use white-out to create more blank writing space from pages without substantive information.

Regardless of such strategies, there's no substitute for reading all the chapters intently and repeatedly. Some more than others, of course. Some chapters seem to be in the book mostly to lay a foundation for other, more-relevant and testable, parts. For example, probably the main reason the study guide has such an extensive discussion of suretyships and bonds in ch. 16 is because they test your understanding of the requirement that *notaries* buy a surety bond (p. 66 in ch. 7). And ch. 18 on mortgages is important to lay the foundation for its application to notary practice in ch. 21. Most of the actual questions are likely to be drawn from the part that most clearly relates to notary law. But it's still useful to write cross-references to the more general discussion so that, on test day, you can easily find the related points if they do ask about them.

It may sound trite to say the best study tip is to study hard, but anyone who offers some magic solution otherwise isn't being honest with you. Fortunately, as the previous section introduced, studying hard is not about memorizing every rule or nuance—you're allowed to find those during the exam—but more about understanding the concepts, contexts, and organization of the study guide so cold that you know what you're looking for even if you don't have it committed to memory.

To build on an example above, there's no need to know by heart all the instances in which Orleans Parish practice differs from the rest of the state. It's OK if you've conceptualized why that may be true, and made a handy list of pages relevant to "Orleans." Answering any question that turns on the location is a matter of pinpointing it from such indexing. The same could be said for all the rules about when acts or forms need to be *recorded* in the clerk's office, not just signed at the notary's office. They tend to ask several questions, most likely three to five, that turn on recordation rules.

If anything, you may need to remind yourself during the test, rather than relying on memory, to search for a confirmation in the study guide of a rule you *think* you know. They can easily make the answer turn on some rule that actually has an exception, which you'd see if you double-check in the relevant places. Or the actual rule is counterintuitive, the opposite of something you thought you've known all along, e.g., doesn't the Secretary of State appoint the notary? Is our civil code "Napoleonic"? (No and no.) At worst, a quick look confirms your memory was right and gives you confidence for the next question. You don't want to spend more than a couple minutes confirming the easier answers—save time for the rest of the exam—but it's smart to check even the most "obvious" ones.

How Much Time on Questions?

You should similarly go into the exam with a plan for how long you spend on any one question. Commit to spending no more than three or four minutes even on the hardest question, mark your best guess, move on, and come back to that one if you have time. 300 minutes divided by 75 questions is 4. Some easier questions (like that "heir" is used for an "intestate" testament) take far less and buy time, but you also may need time for a bathroom break or two and a water-fountain sortie.

Of course you won't waste focus actually timing each question, but you certainly can get a feeling that you're lingering on a hard one. It's better to return to it later than not to finish the exam, missing the chance at several closing questions. Meanwhile, though, fill in the dot of your best effort for those four minutes (you probably did at least eliminate some answers and so increased your odds), even if you think you'll come back to that one later. Don't make a habit of leaving blank circles along the way. You can change the answer if you're sure you did it wrong the first time around—basically, only if you see the correct answer in the book itself or you realize a clear reason your guess was wrong. Otherwise, leave your four-minute answer alone.

In addition to the standard tip not to linger too long on a hard question, ULL's Fred Davis has made the larger point that you don't want to fixate on a whole section at the start of the exam if it's bogging you down or freaking you out. Maybe the first 15 are a difficult subject-group for you (e.g., it's on sales and mortgages, which baffles you). So, simply start at Question 16, at a familiar section (say, notary practice) that creates momentum. Everyone apparently gets the same questions that count, but there are at least two versions of the test used in the exam room—such as "A" and "B," to prevent copying—with the questions in different orders. I'd add you probably should not skip too many individual questions as you go, but it makes sense to skip a whole section of 15, to return with some wind at your back.

On any one question, be sure to read all the answer choices and not fixate on the first one that looks right. The examiners emphasize that it's a search for the "best" answer, not one that is right in some technical or limited way. They consciously may include a "distractor" that is OK as far as it goes, or partly right, but doesn't fully resolve the essential issue in the question—and doesn't count. It may be true for a narrow reason when the larger concern you can see they are trying to test by the question as a whole is not met.

To be sure, there are plenty of questions with only one right answer, and this dilemma of the tempting distractor at worst narrows you down to two decent options. So it shouldn't intimidate you too much. Just be aware of how they do that at times and the need to read all choices. This feeds back to the suggestion, above, of noting true or false next to statements in A through D, to keep it all straight as you go.

As challenging as one section of the exam may seem, or the exam as a whole even, keep in mind that there's a decent margin of error to earn a passing score. Since a 70% usually passes, and they'll have as many as 80 questions, you can miss around 24 questions and still pass. Knowing this should ease the pressure some, especially for any one question that risks bogging you down (say, a tough property description one). I recognize that not all of the 80 questions are scored, as some are experimental, but the logic of this *ratio* still applies: if all 80 counted, you'd need to get 56 right, and so on for smaller numbers.

This also means that in a section of 15 questions, and assuming five such groups (a total of 75 questions), you can miss *four* questions in each group and still leave room to miss a couple more here or there, and pass. You can set a realistic goal for any one question, or any one section, and not be overly intimidated.

Passing Score

About a month later, though lately often longer than that, LSU will send your result in a curt email. Officially the passing score is 75% of the questions they count (excluding some experimental or rejected questions they throw in, often to try out for future exams). But they reserve the right to adjust what passes after evaluation of all results and consideration of "post-test statistical analysis." This has meant in recent years that in fact a score of about 70% correct and above is passing. You can't know until you get your score, and they're only promising that a 75% passes, but consistently they do wind up accepting many exams just below that score.

Once you pass, the SOS website suggests the final formal steps you need to go through to be commissioned in your parish of residence. The requirements, covered on study guide pp. 64-68, are not just steps to take but are statutory mandates to learn for the exam itself. Mainly you'll need to file with the Secretary of State an oath of office, proof of a bond or equivalent, and sample signature. Plus pay the SOS again, naturally. Congratulations!

16
Your Notes

Consider writing:
- Exam mistakes I keep making
- Issues with time-management I may have, and ideas to improve
- Areas of law I seem to be misunderstanding
- Tips I need to remember for exam day
- Notes on notary law and practice to write into the study guide
- Encouragement and envisioning a positive outcome: it works in sports

About the author

STEVEN ALAN CHILDRESS is a professor at Tulane Law School, holding the Conrad Meyer III Professorship in Civil Procedure. He has taught Evidence, Torts, and The Legal Profession at Tulane since 1988, in addition to visiting positions at Loyola–New Orleans and George Washington. He also teaches Tulane's undergraduate class in Louisiana Notary Law. He has lectured in Tulane's continuing legal education program on notary law and practice, legal ethics, and evidence, as well as teaching Louisiana Bar Review for a decade.

Alan earned his JD from Harvard and a PhD in Jurisprudence from Berkeley. He clerked in Shreveport for the federal court of appeals, then practiced law in California. He is a member of the Louisiana Notary Association, the Law and Society Association, and the California and D.C. bars. He is in the relatively rare position of having taken both a bar exam and the state notary exam. He co-authored the treatise *Federal Standards of Review*, edited three books on the legal profession, and annotated a 2010 edition of Oliver Wendell Holmes's *The Common Law*. Recently, he authored an affordable and best-selling supplement to the official state text; its current edition is entitled *Louisiana Notary Exam Sidepiece to the 2022 Study Guide*. He has also published an introductory guide, *Become a Notary Public in Louisiana*.

He is a commissioned Louisiana notary with statewide jurisdiction who, with his wife Michele (an attorney-notary since 2002), has owned a notary-and-shipping service in Jefferson Parish. They have performed thousands of notarial acts covering a wide variety of subjects and formats. They also offer affordable notary prep webinars, live and recorded, through *www.notarysidepiece.com*.

If you have suggestions for test-taking advice, corrections to this workbook, or examples where you think the author's strategies can be improved, they are welcome. Please email them to *achildress@tulane.edu*.

Visit us at *www.quidprobooks.com.*

www.ingramcontent.com/pod-product-compliance
Lightning Source LLC
Chambersburg PA
CBHW060301240426
43661CB00060B/2861